働く人のための探偵
米 産業医学の祖
女性医師アリス・ハミルトンを知っていますか？

ステファニー サンマルチノ マクファーソン 著
ジャネット シュルツ 挿絵
東　敏昭　吉村美穂　訳

訳者はじめに

　産業保健の分野に携わる方々はアリス・ハミルトンをご存知でしょうか。本書は、一人の女性産業医学学徒、産業保健実務者の一生を著したものです。本来は欧米英語圏の学童や若い世代の読者を対象とした偉人伝記シリーズの中の一冊として書かれたものです。意志と行動力、リサーチマインドを持つことの大切さを教えてくれるとともに、産業医学・産業保健の分野で生きることの意義とロマンも教えてくれます。

　日本ではあまり知られていませんが、アリス・ハミルトンは、米国の公衆衛生大学院大学ではテキストに必ず出てくる同国産業医学のパイオニアです。特に、米国の歴史よりも古い歴史を持つハーバード大学が200年以上の歴史の後に初めて迎えた医学部女性教授ということも印象的です。准教授ではありましたが終生教授待遇を保証するとして大学側からの強い要請により迎えられました。米国の政府機関である疾病管理センターの傘下の国立労働安全衛生研究所（NIOSH）の中には彼女の名前を冠した研究所もあり、国立労働安全衛生研究所が、その年に最も優れた産業医学関連著作物を現した研究者には彼女の名前を冠した賞を出しています。

　一方で、1970年代に発行された、彼女の業績を称え肖像を印刷した切手には、「社会変革者（social reformer）」と説明がなされています。労働、環境という彼女の取り組んだ課題だけでなく、まだ職業の世界では女性の地位が低い当時の社会で、象牙の

塔といわれる大学が変わり、女性の社会進出を進め、企業の社会的責任の確立を進めていく流れにも貢献したリーダーとしての彼女の業績を認めたものです。彼女が生きた時代、アメリカ合衆国という国が南北戦争後の19世紀後半から20世紀後半まで歩んだ時の流れを追い、2つの大戦があった時代の背景を思い浮かべながら読んでいただければ幸いです。

The Worker's Detective : A Story About Dr.Alice Hamilton
Text copyright © 1992 by Stephanie Sammartino McPherson
Illustrations copyright © 1992 by Carolrhoda Books. Inc.
Published by arrangement with Carolrhoda Books, Inc.,a Division of
Lerner Publishing Group, Minneapolis, Minnesota, U.S.A.
through Japan Foreign-Rights Centre
All rights reserved.

目　次

序　文……………………………………………………… 1

ふたとおりの人間………………………………………… 3

冒険への渇望……………………………………………… 11

医学のミステリー………………………………………… 19

産業医学の草分け………………………………………… 29

地上の危険、地下の危険………………………………… 37

貢献しつづけること……………………………………… 44

あとがき…………………………………………………… 51

　訳者あとがき…………………………………………… 53

　アリス・ハミルトン医学博士………………………… 55

　活動年表 ………………………………………………… 58

　代表的伝記等…………………………………………… 61

　原　文…………………………………………………… 63

序　　文

　アリス・ハミルトンは1869年2月に生まれた。ちょうど南北戦争が終結して、アメリカ合衆国の産業が新たな成長期を迎えようとしていた時代であった。国家は蒸気船の建造や、鉄道網や電信網を拡張することに力を注ぎ、様々な新しい発明は、化学製品や鉄鋼、機械の生産方法を改良していった。電力はパワフルで新しいエネルギー源をもたらしたので、ほどなく工場ではより多くの商品が生産され、以前にも増して、それらの工業製品を容易に出荷することができるようになった。

　一方の変化として、規模が拡大した工場はより多くの労働者を雇うようになったので、街も発展していき、産業はニューイングランドや東海岸からほかの地域へも拡がっていった。この時代の急激な発展と変化は、アメリカやヨーロッパの産業革命として知られている。しかし残念なことに、これらの産業の発達から発生しうる健康への危険性について、ほとんどのアメリカ人は関心を抱くことはなかった。人々は、いろいろな役にたつ新しい商品に目を奪われるだけで、それらを作った労働者たちに目をむけることもなかった。

　しかし、アリス・ハミルトンはそれをすべて変えていった。

ふたとおりの人間

　子供の頃のアリス・ハミルトンは、長いスカートの裾をたくしあげて木製の剣を振り回しながら、いとこたちを追いかけて大はしゃぎだった。まるで英雄だったアーサー王と円卓の騎士たちが勝利を収めたときのように、りんご園にはいつもガチャガチャとおもちゃの武器の音が響いていた。何度同じ場面を繰り返しても子供たちにとっては飽きることがなく、時には、りんご園がシャーウッドの森に早変わりして、ロビンフッドや彼を取り巻く愉快な家来たちに変身したり、またトロイの木馬伝説を蘇らせたりした。何を演じようが、そこには日々の生活をドラマにしてしまう多くの役者たちが揃っていた。

　ハミルトン家の４人姉妹、エディス、アリス、マーガレット、そしてノラの家から、ほんのちょっと離れた場所にいとこ達は住んでいたので、毎日のようにアリスの家へやってきてこんな風にゲームを楽しんだものだった。アリスは、いとこの中でもアグネスとアレンとは年が近く、いつも一緒にいたので、その頭文字を取って「３人組のA」という愛称で呼ばれていた。

　陽気な「３人組のA」とその仲間たちはいつもグループになって、インディアナ州のフォートウェインという町にある同じ敷地内のお互いの家や祖母の住んでいる家に出入りしていた。実業家でフォートウェインの設立者の一人であった祖父は、家族に十分な財産を残していたので、アリスたちの祖母の家はとりわけ大きく立派で、人々から「オールドハウス」と呼ばれていた。

祖母は女性が社会的権利を持つことを強く支持しており、「女性たちは、いつか男性と同等の仕事に就けるわ。そして自分たちに財産所有権や参政権が与えられる時代がきっとくるわ」とよく言っていた。彼女は、女性の権利拡大のための運動を通して知り会った、スーザン・B・アンソニーの良き友達でもあった。アンソニーは婦人参政権を勝ち取るために生涯を捧げたことで有名な女性で、インディアナ州を訪れる時は、いつも祖母のいるオールドハウスに立ち寄って滞在したものだった。

　アリスの母親のガートルード・ハミルトン夫人も祖母と同じように自立した女性で、いつも娘たちに「自分の持っている信念や考えを人前ではっきりと主張しなさい」と教えていた。「世の中には"誰かがあることについて何かをすべき時、どうして私がそれをしなければならないの？"と思う人と"誰かがしなければならないのなら、私がそれをやりましょう"と思う、ふたとおりの人がいるのですよ」。

　母から言われた「ふたとおりの人」という言葉を、アリスはそれからずっと忘れることはなかった。この時アリスは、幼い子供なりに自分がどちらの考えを持つべきなのかを、すでに分かっていた。この世の中を住みよい場所とするために、人々を助けて、何か大切なことをやりたいと望むようになっていたのだった。でもそれは一体何なのかしら？　外の世界をほとんど知らずに育ったひとりの少女にとって、これは難しい問いであった。というのも、ハミルトン家の両親は子供たちを家庭の中だけで教育してきたので、アリスはフォートウェインでは、いとこ達以外の同じ年

頃の子供の姿すら見たことがなかったからだった。アリスたち姉妹は、父親のモンゴメリーからラテン語を、母親のガートルードからフランス語を、そして召使いたちからはドイツ語を学び、歴史や宗教や文学すらも家庭の中で学んだのであった。

　なにしろ休暇を過ごす時でさえ、一般の裕福な家庭の子供たちと比べても違ったものであった。アリスが10歳になった1879年から、毎年夏になるとハミルトン一家はヒューロン湖とミシガン湖が合流する海峡にあるマッキナック島という保養地を訪れていた。家族を乗せたボートが湖畔に近づくにつれ、アリスは森や松の木で覆われた絶壁、砂利の海岸など、いつもの見慣れた風景が何も変わってないことを確かめるように、遠くから目を凝らしたものだった。

　こんなふうに、アリスはマッキナック島とフォートウェインでは、何不自由ない少女時代を送ってきたが、成長するにしたがって彼女の中の何かが変わり始めていた。それはアリスが14歳の時、いとこのアレンがボストンの学校に通うようになってからだった。アレンはアリスへの手紙の中に、自分の勉強している科学のことを書き綴っていたが、特に物理学について書かれてあったものを読んだとき、アリスの心は大きく揺れた。そして自分も物理学を学んでみたいと思い、父親にそのことを話したことがあったが、銀行員でもあり食料雑貨の卸売業も営んでいた父親にとって科学は無縁の世界だった。「百科事典でも十分勉強はできる」と父親は言った。それはそれで正しかったが、ただ一つ困ったことに、アリスには事典に書かれた専門的用語や記述の意味がほとん

ど理解できなかった。

　それから１年後、アリスは科学ではなく「医学」という分野を知るきっかけとなった『マーブオアシス』という最も興味をそそられる一冊の本と出会った。それは、ある外交官がペルシャを旅行した時のことを綴った日記であったが、それを読んだアリスは、どこか遠い国に冒険に出て、そこで出会うかもしれない病に伏している人や貧困にあえぐ人々を助けるために、医学の伝道師となって活躍している自分自身の姿を空想してみた。アリスはこのようにたくさんの夢や希望を持ってはいたが、医学を勉強する準備は何もできていなかった。

　２年のちの1886年、両親はアリスをコネチカット州にある寄宿制の女子学校に入学させた。その学校では語学や哲学を学んだが、クラスメイトを通して学んだことは授業よりももっと貴重なものだった。クラスメイトたちと日課の散歩をする時、いつも長い時間おしゃべりをした。新しく友達になった子のほとんどは、この学校に入る以前にも別の学校に通っていたので多くの友人がいたし、いろんな経験も豊富だった。そんな話を聞いているうちに、アリスは自分の過ごしてきた子供時代が友人たちとは違っていたことに気づき始めていた。

　そして、フォートウェインに戻った時、アリスはもっと広い世界と向き合っていきたいと熱望する若い女性に成長していた。彼女は２歳になる弟のアーサーが加わった新しい家族に会うのをとても楽しみにしていた。自分自身も結婚して子供を持つ年齢に達していたが、恋愛や結婚より何か仕事を持つことに関心を抱いて

いたのだった。

　そして姉のエディスと将来について話していた時、医師になりたいと打ち明けた。エディスもまたアリスと同様に、自分自身の仕事を持ちたいと考えていたが、妹が迷うことなく自分の行きたい道を選んだことに驚き、また両親もアリスの出した決断を心配した。というのも、このころエリザベス・ブラックウェルがアメリカで最初の女性医師になってから40年もの歳月が流れていたが、まだ多くの人々は医師という職業は女性には不向きであると考えていた時代であったからだった。ブラックウェル博士が医師としての歴史を刻んで数十年の間に4,500人もの女性が医学の学位を取得したが、医師としての役割の機会を得ることは男性医師ほど多くはなかった。そういうこともあり、アリスは自分の出した決断については慎重になっていたが、その目標を断念するようなことはなかった。

　「たとえどんなに遠い場所でも、そこがスラム街であっても、私は医師として行くべき所へ行くつもりです。そしてどこへ行っても必ず人の役に立つようになります。私は人種やそれぞれに置かれている状況の区別なく、あらゆる人にも会うべきだと思っています。だから学校で時間に拘束されて仕事をしている教師*や、上役の下で働かねばならない看護婦*のような職業ではだめなのです」と考えていた。

　アリスはそれから医学校に入るための必要な科学の知識を勉強

　＊註：19世紀末のアメリカの社会においての表現です。

し始めた。そのやる気と頑張りにより、両親は娘が医師になることを最終的に納得せざるを得なかった。

　1890年、21歳になったアリスは懸命な努力の末、地方の小さな学校から、国内でトップランクの医学校のひとつとして知られていたミシガン大学への入学を許可された。そしてそこで、わずか13名の女子学生のひとりとなったのであった。

冒険への渇望

　顕微鏡の中のピンクやブルーに染まった細胞の姿にアリスは集中していた。同じように他の学生たちも顕微鏡に目を凝らしていたが、教室には皆に行きわたるだけの充分な数の顕微鏡がなかったので、アリスは授業の始まる前のまだ誰もいない教室に来て、自分専用の顕微鏡を確保することが楽しみであった。レンズを通して生命の基本構造である細胞を見ることは、アリスにとって何よりも魅惑的なものであった。組織学の授業では正常な状態の細胞を識別することを学び、病理学の授業では異常な細胞の標本を検査した。アリスはとても勤勉な学生だったので、授業で習うことの一つひとつを吸収していった。

　1893年に医学の学位を取得した時、アリスは病気の原因を最も基礎的な角度から研究したいと思っていたので、これからの人生を病理学の研究に捧げようと決心していた。人が病気になると影響を受ける細胞があることを学び、「何が原因でこれらの正常な細胞が変化し、死に至ってしまうのだろうか？」、「それらの細胞は病気の症状によってどのように変化するのだろうか？」という疑問に、研究室で細胞を研究することによって答えを見出したいと思っていた。しかしアリスには、インターンとしての任務が残っていた。これは、実際に患者たちと接する経験を提供し、卒業後もこれから自分が生涯やっていける仕事を見つけるのに役だつものであった。

　その年の夏、教育課程が始まるので、アリスはいつもより早く

休暇先のマッキナック島を発たなければならなかった。父親が本土に向かってボートを漕ぐにつれ、島がだんだん小さくなるのを見たとき、アリスはすでにホームシックになっていた。インターンとしてのこの年は一体どんなものになるのだろう、私は患者を適切に処置できるのかしら？

　間もなくアリスは着任し、激務をこなした。職場はミネアポリスにある女性と子供のために作られたノースウェスタン病院で、そこでは患者の診察や薬の調合、そして新生児を分娩させるということまで、すべてひとりでこなさねばならなかった。これまでずっと先輩医師たちが行ってきたこのような非科学的な方法は、アリスの仕事を決して楽にすることはなかった。のちに従妹のアグネスに宛てた手紙の中で、彼女は自分の失望感をこう記している。「私がこれまでとても大事だと教えられてきた、すべてに正確で注意深くきめ細やかな作業というのは、ここでは全然通用しません。いつでも即座に診断して迅速に処方箋を作り、決して取り乱したりしないで緊急事態に対処しなければならないのです。私にできることなんて何もありません。ここには研究室すらないし、顕微鏡だって私が持っていたような質の良いものではありません」。

　このような厳しい状況にいるにもかかわらず、アリスは次第に患者たちの役に立っていると自覚するようになっていた。しかしそれから2ヶ月のちに、ボストンでの別のインターンの仕事を提供されたので、ノースウェスタン病院を離れることを決意した。アリスはミネアポリスにあるこの病院ではいつも一人作業で寂し

い思いをしていたが、新しい職場であるニューイングランド病院の評判は良かった。この病院も同じく女性と子供の患者を対象とする病院だった（この頃はまだ、女性医師が男性患者を診ることは不相応なことだと考えられていた時代であった）。

　ボストンに到着して最初に配属されたのは産科病棟であった。アリスはたくさんの健康な赤ん坊を分娩させたが、時には生まれて間もない乳幼児の命を助けられなかったり、母親の苦痛を和らげることが出来なかったこともあった。ある時、まだかなり若い母親が出産後に死亡した時、アリスは深い悲しみに陥った。そして、臨床医として働くよりも研究室にいる方が自分には合っているのではないかしらと彼女は思い始めていた。患者を診ることによって引き起されるストレスで感情を乱されることに、アリスは困惑するばかりだった。

　それから数ヶ月後、アリスは貧しい人たちのための低料金の診療所へ転任した。ここでの新しい任務は往診をすることだったが、陰気な地下室や狭い屋根裏部屋、そして酒場の奥にある小部屋などに出向いて診療をしなければならず、それは想像もしなかったことだった。時にはボストンのスラム街の隅々まで歩いて往診し、真夜中まで自宅に戻らない日もあった。

　往診先には失業中の移民たちが多く住んでいて、食料や衣類が不足していたり、部屋を暖めるための石炭すらないような家を訪問することがたびたびあった。アリスはそんな貧しい家族に地元の慈善施設を紹介したりした。このように些細ではあるが、自ら出向いていくというやり方で、アリスはこれまでとは違った自分

の世界を築いていったのだった。

　ラシェル・スロボディンスキーもまた、世の中を変えようと決意していたインターンのひとりだった。ロシア生まれのラシェルは17歳の時に故郷を離れてニューヨークへ渡った。そこでは、ある労働条件の悪い工場で仕事を得たが、その小さな工場の中は蒸し暑く不衛生で、従業員たちは長時間の労働を強いられており、しかも賃金は極めて低かった。アリスはそんなラシェルの話に仰天しつつも次第に魅了され、「ねえ、私にすべて教えて！」とこの新しい友人に懇願した。

　最初アリスは、自分が私立の学校で楽しく過ごしていた頃、ラシェルはすでに生活のために働いていたことを知って、自分が何の不自由もない幸せな子供時代を送ってきたことを恥ずかしく思っていた。「ラシェルは同世代なのに、私たちが60歳になるときまでに経験するかもしれないことよりも、もっとたくさんの試練を切り抜けてきたような女性です」と、アリスはアグネスへの手紙に綴った。

　1894年、アリスはインターンを終えたが開業医になるつもりはなく、ラシェルがやっているような困難に直面している人々を助けたいと強く願うようになっていた。そして病理学と社会福祉とを結び付けて仕事や研究をすることが出来ないだろうかと考えていた。そんな時、アリスを指導していた教授たちから、病理学が最も進んでいるドイツで基礎医学の勉強をしてみないかと勧められた。ちょうど姉のエディスがペンシルベニアのブリンマウル大学の文学部を卒業した後にドイツへの留学を計画していたの

で、アリスにとってはまたとない話だった。翌年の1895年、ふたりの姉妹はドイツへ旅立つ準備のために故郷のフォートウェインへ戻った。

　そしてせわしく旅の計画を立てていたある日、一番末の妹のノラが部屋に突然飛び込んできて興奮気味に言った。「今夜、ジェーン・アダムスがフォートウェインで講演をするらしいわ」。ジェーン・アダムスですって！　あのハルハウスの創立者がフォートウェインへ来てくれるなんて！　アダムスはシカゴの貧民街にハルハウスという厚生施設を建てて、人々のために食料や避難所など必要なものを支援してきた女性であった。アリスはまだそこへ行ったことはなかったが、ハルハウスではアダムスや住込みのボランティアたちが、いつでも貧しい移民労働者たちやその家族を受け入れていることなど、彼女の行ってきた数々の有名な社会的活動についてはよく知っていた。

　その夜、3人の姉妹はジェーン・アダムスの講演会へ出席した。そこでのアダムスの話に感銘を受けたアリスは、自分こそが彼女と目標を共有していると実感した。そして実験室での研究と社会福祉事業とを両立させる完璧な方法を思い立った。それは病理学者としての研究を続けながら、夜間と週末は厚生施設で働くという方法であった。

　アダムスの講演を聞いてまもなく、アリスは姉のエディスとともにドイツへ旅立ち、最初にライプチヒ、のちにミュンヘンで研究を行った。そこではドイツ人の友人が出来て楽しく過ごしていたが、まだよく知らない病理のことについてはあまり学ぶことは

なかった。授業では、女性は"透明人間"のようなものだった。特別な講義に出席するには他の男性医師たちが入ってくる前に、女性たちは先輩医師によって部屋の隅の椅子まで連れていかれる。そしてどこへ行ってもいつも同じ質問を浴びせられた。「もしアメリカの女性が科学の世界に入ったら、誰が靴下を繕う仕事をするのですか？」と。

　その後、アリスはアメリカに戻ってきた時、仕事が見つからなかったのでバルチモアにあるジョンズ・ホプキンス大学で病理の研究を続けていた。1年後の1897年、彼女はシカゴのノースウェスタン女子医科大学の教授として迎えられた。そしてアリスは、このシカゴこそが、自分が生活したいと思っていた場所だわ！と思った。

　不安と期待を胸に、アリスはジェーン・アダムスに会うためハルハウスへ向かった。アリスが想像していたとおり、アダムスは思いやりのある親切な女性だった。しかし残念なことにハルハウスはすでに他のボランティアたちで埋め尽くされ、アリスが使える部屋は残っていなかった。しかし彼女は立ち止まってひと息つくことなくハルハウスをあとにして、北へ数マイル離れた「コモンズ」と呼ばれる別の施設を訪ねたが、ここでも同じようにもぐり込むことはできず、引き返さざるを得なかった。疲労と失望の中で、アリスは研究と社会福祉活動を両立させるという目標をどうすれば達成できるだろうかと考え続けていた。

　その年の夏、アリスは休養をとるために静かで美しいマッキナック島へ戻った。彼女は医療活動だけでは、自分がやろうとして

いる冒険への渇望を満たしてはくれないことを知っていたが、自分の未来に確信を持って生きていた。そしてある朝のこと、郵便船が島にやって来て一通の手紙を届けてくれた。それはジェーン・アダムスからであった。その手紙にハルハウスの部屋にやっと空きができたことが書かれており、アリスは胸を躍らせた。その年の10月にこの若い医師は、ついに念願の施設で人生をスタートさせることができたのであった。

医学のミステリー

　ハルハウスの優雅なデザインと高い天井は、いろいろな意味で故郷のオールドハウスを思い出させるものがあった。しかしこの古くて素敵な施設での生活は、あらゆることから保護されていた子供時代とはほど遠いものだった。ボストンで仕事をしていた時、アリスは貧困というものをさんざん見てきたが、このシカゴではその貧困のど真ん中で生活することになった。

　ハルハウスを頼ってきた人々は、わずかな報酬をもらって工場で長時間働かねばならない労働者ばかりであった。彼らはひしめき合った安アパートの中の狭くて風通しの悪い部屋に住んでおり、建物のまわりにはネズミがちょろちょろと駆け回り、ゴミ箱は悪臭を放っているような状態であった。

　患者たちは近所に住んでいる顔なじみの人々でもあったので、ボストンで接してきた患者よりも彼らの希望や苦労をずっと深く理解することができた。アリスはここのすべての人々を救いたいと切望し、病気の子供を往診したり、乳幼児の健康診断や入浴をすることの出来る診療所を設立した。そこでは、人々に病気の予防法についても教えようと試みたが、容易なことではなかった。若い母親たちは、バクテリアがどのように繁殖するのかということも理解できなかった。また、30歳という年齢のアリスが、人々の目には経験を積んだ専門家にはとても見えなかったようだった。しかし彼女の穏やかな微笑みや優しい心遣いは、子供たちと同じようにその両親たちをも惹きつけるものがあった。

アリスは住人たちの健康を気遣うことのほかに、彼らの生活をも豊かにしたいと願い、美術や英語を学ぶための夜間教室を開いたり、少年たちのクラブ活動や男性用のアスレチッククラブでも熱心に指導にあたった。また週末には子供たちを郊外へピクニックに連れていくのを楽しんだ。そんなアリスのまわりには、いつも子供たちの姿があった。ハルハウスの通りをせわしく働いている彼女のあとを、明るくて活発な子供たちがわいわい騒ぎながらくっついて回った。この子供たちが幸せな人生を送ることを、彼女はどれほど強く願っていたことだろうか。

　子供たちの両親がより高い賃金と労働時間短縮を求めるストライキをすることがあったが、アリスも時には一緒にデモに参加したりした。そのような行為は逮捕される危険性もあったが、アリスはプラカードを高く掲げて労働者たちと工場の前を行きつ戻りつ行進したものだった。

　ハルハウスで5年間ほど過ごした頃、アリスが教鞭を取っていたノースウェスタン女子医科大学は男子大学の一部となった。新しく共学となった大学では、アリスのやる仕事はなくなってしまったので、彼女は感染症記念研究所というところで、細菌学者としての新しい仕事を見つけた。しかし研究所の仕事よりもハルハウスで過ごすことのほうが、アリスにはずっと得るものが多かった。

　ハルハウスで工場労働者と顔見知りになればなるほど、彼らは自らの病気や身体的不調についてアリスに話してくれるようになった。作業員たちの話を聞いていると、彼らの身体が憂慮すべき

状態にあることが分かり始めた。それらの症状は、血色の悪さや栄養不良、皮膚の皺などで、また、塗装業者や鉛工場の作業員たちは消化不良に悩まされており、手首を動かすのにも支障をきたしていた。それらはすべて鉛中毒の症状であった。製鉄工場で働く作業員は一酸化炭素を吸入しており、家畜飼育場の作業員には肺炎やリウマチを患っている率が高いことが分かった。何人かの人々は、このような症状は何かの病気が原因だと思っていたが、アリスは工場のお粗末な作業環境が彼らの健康を損ねているのではないかという疑問を抱いていた。

　1907年、そんなアリスの疑問を裏付けたのは、トーマス・オリバーの『危険な職業』というタイトルの一冊の本だった。そこには、特定の職業が引き起こす健康リスクについて多くのことが書かれていた。トーマス・オリバーは、英国の産業社会の調査に貢献していた人物だった。その本を読み終えたとき、アリスはアメリカの工場について書かれたものを調べてみようと考えた。

　しかし驚いたことに、アメリカの産業社会について書いた文献を見つけることができなかった。他の医師たちにも協力を求めてみたが、そこでもまた、アメリカの労働者は産業中毒など被ってはないと断言され、アリスは唖然としたのだった。

　アリスはハルハウスで永く暮らしていたので、このような安直な答えを受け入れるわけにはいかなかった。実際、彼女のまわりのアメリカ人作業員たちは、何らかの病を患っていたり、時には死に至っている。ただ自分の仕事をしていただけだというのに！

　何とかしなければならない、今アメリカの工場で起こっている

この事実を誰かが証明しなければならない、とアリスは思った。いくつかの州では労働者の健康を守るための法律が通っていたが、ほとんどの州ではそこまで至っていなかった。この時アリスは、自分が新しい未知の分野に踏み出しているのを感じていた。
　アリスは作業員たちの話を聞いて、その不可解な病気についてあらゆる手がかりを調査し続けた。そして1908年9月、アメリカ人のより良い職場環境を立て直すための、彼女にとって初めての論文を出版した。また、女性の健康問題についても取り組んだ。鉛を取り扱う仕事に従事する女性労働者は、同じ職種に就く男性労働者よりも深刻な問題をかかえているのではないかとアリスは考えていたからだった。そして、女性は洗濯工場や缶詰工場など、高温かつ湿度の高い場所で作業することが多かったが、このような作業環境は心臓病や結核の危険性を高め、妊婦は流産を引き起こす危険性もあった。まもなく多くの人々がアリスの関心事を知るようになったが、彼女の説に裏付けを与えられる者はほとんどいなかった。
　そして、アリスが39歳の時、彼女に重要な根拠を示すために、ジョン・アンドリュースという医師がハルハウスを訪れた。アンドリュースは「燐壊死」と呼ばれる奇妙な病気の研究をしていた。その病気は顔の骨が削げ落ち、ひどい痛みを伴いながら腫れ上がるもので、重い症状になると目や顎の骨を失うこともある恐ろしい病気だった。それは、マッチ工場で働くある限られた人々の集団だけが、その病気に罹る危険性にさらされていた。燐壊死という病気の原因は、作業中に吸いこむリン化合物に関係していた。

アリスはアンドリュースの持ってきた燐壊死という病気に関してのリポートを熟読したが、他の医学の専門家たちは、これまでアメリカでそんな病気は知られていないと主張した。しかしアンドリュースは、彼らこそが間違っていることを証明した。アメリカのマッチ工場労働者に150例以上もの燐壊死があることを突き止めたのだった。アリスもこの知見を人々の教育に役立てたり、医学界の関心をかきたてたりした。

　そしてその論文発表がなされて2年間のうちに、マッチ製造におけるリン化合物の使用を禁止する新しい法律が出来た。リン化合物の代わりに亜硫化物と呼ばれる新しい物質が急速に使われるようになり、まもなく燐壊死は過去の病気となったのだった。

　アリス・ハミルトン、ジョン・アンドリュース、そして他の研究者たちの成果は、アメリカの産業にゆっくりと変化をもたらした。1908年12月、イリノイ州の知事は職業病委員会を設立した。アリスは既にその分野では専門家として認められていたので、その委員会の9人の委員のひとりとして任命された。そして委員会の中では、誰よりも産業医学に関して造詣が深かったので、調査の責任者になるように依頼された。同時に専門家たちは産業衛生を研究し、イリノイ州の工場における危険な職業のリストを作り始めた。

　アリスはこれからこの仕事に挑戦しようと決意を固めていたが、同時に困惑させられることも多かった。というのは、イリノイ州の労働者たちは、自分たちの直面している職業の危険性について何も気づいていなかったからだった。アリスは自分がこの仕

事を続けていくことによって、彼らが気づくことをただただ願うばかりだった。

　研究室から離れることによって、アリスはようやく納得のいく仕事ができた。彼女が特に進めていた調査は鉛中毒に関するものだったが、それは最初予想していた以上に広範囲にわたるもので、イリノイ州のすべての工場を巡回して鉛に曝露されていると考えられる仕事に従事する作業員たちに聞き取り調査を行った。

「あなたの仕事で一番つらいものはなんですか？」

「ここでどのくらい働いていますか？」

「この仕事を始めたときと同じように今も健康ですか？」

　このような質問は作業者たちを驚かせるものだった。というのも、彼らは今まで自分たちの生活について他人からこんな風に関心を持たれたことがなかったからだった。こんな質問に答えると職を失うのではないかと恐れたりする作業員もいたが、次第にアリスの温かい心遣いに応えるかのように、自分の仕事や体調について語り始めた。

　しかし、アリスは工場訪問から得た以上にもっと多くの情報が欲しかったので、イリノイ州のすべての病院で患者の病歴を長時間かけて調べることにした。そしてその中で鉛中毒に罹った患者の例を見つけると、その人の家を訪問して家族とも話をしたりした。彼らの多くは移民で、身寄りもなく途方にくれていた。アリスは彼らの身に起こっている危険性について教え悟らせようとした。

　ある家を訪問した時に、強い胃痛と手の震えという症状に苦し

むひとりの男性に出くわしてアリスは戸惑っていた。病院での記録を調べて彼は鉛中毒に罹っているのだろうと推測したが、その原因が何であるのかは不明だった。そこでこの男性から詳しく話を聞いてみると、彼は浴槽にエナメル（ほうろう）を塗る作業をしていると言ったのだが、それはアリスが連想していた大量の鉛の曝露が原因で発生するという職種ではなかった。

　そして調査に着手してみると、粉にしたエナメルを浴槽に散布する仕事をしている作業員がいることをつきとめた。その浴槽は白い粒子になったエナメルが溶けるほど温度を高くしてあったので、作業員たちはエナメル粉じんで充満した空気を吸い込まざるを得なかったのだ。

　アリスは自分がやっている調査について説明すると、作業員の1人が粉じんのサンプルを提供してくれたので、スムーズに調査が出来た。研究室で粉じんを調べてみると、エナメルが20パーセントの鉛を含んでいることが分かり愕然としたが、この時代、もっと研究が進歩していたヨーロッパ人ですらこれに気づいてはいなかった。もはやこの病気はミステリーではなくなった。アリスは確信を持ってエナメル塗装を危険な職業のリストに加えた。

　この調査に関わりを持った人の誰もが、調べてきたことを報告するだけであった。アリスが見い出した状況を変えるために何かをしてくれることなど期待できなかった。しかし、職場の改善が行われるまでに一体どのくらいの人々が健康を害することになるのだろうか。今こそ誰かが声を上げねばならない時がきていた。そんなとき、アリスは子供の頃に母親から教えられた「ふたとお

りの人」という言葉を思い出していた。アリスは、これまで調べてきたものを報告するだけでは充分でないことを実感していたので、自分の仕事の範囲ではなかったが、工場での作業環境を改善するよう雇用者たちの説得にも努めた。ある日、エドワード・コーニッシュという、シカゴにいくつもの工場をもつ国立鉛工場の副社長と会う機会があった。その時アリスは、「あなたの工場で働く作業員たちが作業中に鉛によって健康を害しているようです」と勇気をもって伝えた。最初、コーニッシュは彼女の訴えに気分を害していたが、それにも関わらず彼女の優しさと真摯な態度に心を打たれ、ついには「私はあなたの言っていることが正しいとは思えないが、あなたのしようとしていることは理解できます。作業員たちが鉛に曝露されていることを証明できるのなら、あなたの要請に全面的に応えましょう」と言ってくれたのである。

　これに挑戦するかのように、アリスは工場の労働者の間で22例もの鉛中毒の症例を見つけて、自分の調査能力を示してみせた。このことは、コーニッシュを驚ろかせて感銘を与えた。そして彼は、工場の作業環境の改善をアリスに約束してくれたのだった。

産業医学の草分け

　まるで本物の探偵のように、アリスは労働者の病気とその職業の関連を明らかにするため、あらゆる糸口を追跡していった。「この職業病を調べる仕事は、まるでこれからジャングルの中に道をつけるようなもので、入口すら見つけられません」と、彼女は1910年に記している。そしてアリスは、独自に突破口を開いていった。翌年１月に職業病協会の委員会が報告書を発表する前に、アリスは77種の鉛関連企業を対象に500例を超える鉛中毒症例の報告書を提出したのである。

　委員会も明らかにできなかったその確かな根拠に応えるかのように、イリノイ州議会は同年、職業病法を承認した。その法律が作られてからは、工場の雇用者は安全上の留意事項に従い、危険な物質を取り扱う労働者たちのために毎月の健康診断を実施しなくてはならなくなった。他の６つの州も、その年に職業病関連法を承認した。これはすばらしい進歩だったが、アリスは他にもっとやるべきことがあることに気づいていた。もしアメリカの医学の専門家たちが以前から産業界にもっと関心を払っていたら、アリスの仕事はもっと楽になっていたに違いない。

　委員会のメンバーも、同様にそのことに気づいていた。そして委員会では、この分野のより進歩した研究を学ばせるため、アリスをベルギーのブリュッセルで開催される「労働災害と疾病に関する国際会議」へ出席させることにした。アリスにとって、これはまたとない機会だったが、自分の研究時間が奪われることは免

れない。しかし彼女は、病理学より産業医学の分野により貢献できると信じたので、その会議に出席することを熱望した。

　ブリュッセルの会議では、著名なヨーロッパの専門家たちから、産業医学のあらゆる側面からの話を聞くことができた。アリスもまたそこで講演したが、それはある塗料に使用された白い鉛含有物質についての研究発表であった。ヨーロッパの医師たちはアリスの発表に大変興味を示し質問を始めた。「他の職種では鉛中毒の割合はどのくらいですか？」、「危険な職業のための法律規制はありますか？」と。

　しかし面目ないことに、これらの質問に対する答えをアリスは何ひとつ持っていなかった。そしてついには、ベルギーから参加していたひとりの医師が放った言葉で、この議論は終結した。「アメリカには産業衛生が存在しないことがよく分かりました」。アリスは決まり悪くなって顔が火照っていくのを感じていた。

　当惑したのはアリスだけではなく、チャールズ・オニールもそうだった。合衆国の労働委員でもあるオニールは、その会議に出席していた数少ないアメリカ人の一人であった。そしてアリスがアメリカに帰国してすぐ、オニールからの手紙が届いた。それは「これまであなたがイリノイ州のためにやってきたことを、このアメリカすべての州でやってはもらえないだろうか？」という大変重要な要請であった。

　この時アリスは42歳になっており、人生の分岐点に立っていた。新しい任務につけば、いつ研究室へ戻れるのかも分からなかったし、連邦調査員という仕事は彼女にとっては何の名誉でもな

く、多くの責任を課せられることも知っていた。調査は独力で問題のある工場を見つけだして認定しなければならなかったし、工場主に頼んで作業場の中に入れてもらい、どのように作業を進めていくかのガイドラインを作る必要もあった。しかもそれぞれの報告書を提出するまでは給料をもらえない。

　これはつらい条件のように思えたが、産業医学というものはアリスにとって大変重要なことだったので、この絶好のチャンスを断ることなどできなかった。アリスはワシントンでその職位についたあと研究所に戻ることはなかったが、ハルハウスには以前のように通い続けた。新しい仕事は東部から中西部にまで及んだが、ハルハウスを自らの落ちつくべき場所と考え、可能な限りそこで過ごすよう努めた。また、アリスの研究への献身と情熱を理解しているハルハウスの友人の元に帰るのはいつも楽しみなことだった。

　最初の国の調査として、アリスは再び鉛問題を選択し、それらの工場を探し出して訪問することに取りかかった。これらの工場の現場監督の何人かは、よそ者が入り込んできて、工場の管理についてあれこれと非難されることに激怒する者もいた。アリスが女性であることで、その怒りを和げるということもなかった。しかしアリスは彼らを助けるためにここへ来たのであって、けっして憤慨させるためではなく、労働者たちが幸せで健康になれば工場の生産もうまくいくということを指摘したかったのだ。彼女はとてもおだやかで、また誠実で礼儀正しかったので、次第に工場主たちもアリスが自分たちの味方であると認めるようになった。

そしてついには彼女の調査を受け入れ、次から次へと工場の扉が開いていった。

しかし調査していくにしたがって、どの工場も最も基本的な健康水準にも達していないことがわかった。アリスの行く先々で、鉛まみれの手で昼御飯を食べていたり、髪の毛に鉛がべたべたとくっついている従業員の姿があちらこちらで見かけられた。そして、もっともひどかったのが、危険な鉛の粉塵や煙を吸い込んで作業しているのを見た時だった。

アリスはその作業環境のひどさに時には腹立たしく思ったが、いつも平静さを保つようにしていた。というのは、目にするものがどうであれ、アリスはそこの工場主が、シカゴで出会ったエドワード・コーニッシがそうであったように、従業員の健康を気にかけてくれると信じていたからである。そこでアリスは工場内を視察したあと、作業場の設備を整える必要があると工場主や管理者たちを説得した。例えば、作業場に新鮮な空気を送り、粉じんを最小限にするための換気扇や通気孔の使い方などを指導したりした。またすべての労働者に定期的な健康チェックを実施することも強く勧めた。

男性がまだ医学界を支配していた時代だったが、アリスは、むしろ女性であるがゆえに産業衛生を変革することができると感じていた。「もし私が男性だったら、雇用者も医者も今よりもずっと喜んでわたしの話を聞きに来たでしょう」と、アリスは後になって記している。「女性が、その製品の価値よりも、それを生産している労働者の健康のほうにこそ気を遣うのは、自然で正しいこと

のように思えます」。

　鉛について5年間研究したのち、アリスはゴム製品を取り扱う工場の調査を始めた。しかし大変な問題が発生した。ヨーロッパで第一次世界大戦が勃発したのだった。人々の生活のために休む間もなく働いていたアリスは、戦場で若者たちの命が奪われていくことにショックを受けた。

　アリスは、ヨーロッパの平和を願う気持ちをジェーン・アダムスとともに共有していた。1915年、有名な社会学者であるアダムスは「戦争に反対する女性のための国際会議」に参加することを決めたので、アリスも彼女と一緒にオランダに旅立つ計画をたてた。

　二人がオランダのハーグに到着した時、ちょうど最初のセッションが始まろうとしていた。12の参戦国と中立国から1,100人の人々が会議に出席していた。アメリカ人を含むほとんどの女性参加者は、母国でまだ選挙権を持っていなかった。彼女たちは宣戦布告にはいかなる関与もできなかったが、戦争を止めさせるためであれば何でもする意志があった。

　ジェーン・アダムスがフランス、ドイツ、オーストリア・ハンガリー、イタリア、オランダ、そしてスイスの政府の指導者たちを訪れるように要請された時、アリスも非公式の同伴者として同行した。そして戦争を終結させたいという一個人の訴えが失敗に終わって失望しつつ、アリスはアメリカに帰国した。しかし、兵士たちを守るために出来ることは何もなかったが、他にも助けることが出来る人々の集団があった。その人々とは、急速に発展し

つつある軍用品や兵器を製造する工場で働く労働者たちだった。アリスは以前にも増して強い決意を持って、これらの人々に注意を向け始めていた。

地上の危険、地下の危険

　悪臭を放った赤い煙に追いかけられるように、アリスは野原を横切って走り出した。彼女は息苦しさを感じて、はあはあと喘ぎながらピクリン酸工場から排出されている有害な煙から逃れようとした。その有害な化学物質は弾薬を製造するために使用されているものだった。

　アリスはふと気がつくと茎が枯れているとうもろこし畑の中にいた。かつてその土地を耕作していた人々は、今や戦争のための化学製品を作る工場で働いていた。この時、アメリカはまだ第一次世界大戦に参戦していなかったが、戦争のために必要な爆弾等をフランスへ供給していたのであった。今回のような工場の事故は、放棄された土地に残っていた作物までも台無しにしていた。

　アリスの周囲のあちこちで、毒性の煙が建物に充満し始めると、工場の中から従業員たちが慌てて逃げ出してきた。彼らのほとんどは、毎日の作業中にピクリン酸を浴びて身体中が黄色に染められていたので、街の人々からカナリアと呼ばれていた。

　アリスはほんの数時間前に、ニュージャージーの鉄道の駅で初めてそのカナリアと呼ばれる人々の集団を見ていたので、汚染された雲が空の中に消えていくのを見た時、駅で出会ったある男を思い出していた。その男は黒人で、爪と毛髪と眉毛は明るいオレンジ色をしており、頬と手の平は鮮やかな黄色に染められていた。「工場は危険ではありませんか」と、アリスはその男に尋ねた。

「黄色い原料が原因じゃないとは言えないが」と、彼は答えた。「だけど黄色い原料を作っている時は赤い煙が流れ出して、それを吸い込むと倒れちまう。逃げなければ、つかまっちまうんだ。その時怪しいと思わなくても、家に帰って普段どおりに夕飯喰って床に就いたあとで、息苦しくなって、朝までには死んじまうんだよ」。

　アリスは、他の工場でも同じような荒れ放題の状況を目のあたりにした。ヴァージニア州の無煙火薬工場でも、火薬の微粒子が大きなパイプから容器に注がれるのを見た。それは何の害も及ぼさないように見えたが、工場を案内してくれた従業員は、粒子がこすれると時々火花を散らすのだと説明した。そして「もしそんなことが起こったら、一番近い窓に向かって走るんだよ」と彼は注意した。アリスは目を見張った。3階の窓から飛び降りるのですって？　その窓から地面へ向かってのびる長い避難用の滑り台があったが、幸いこの時はそれを使う必要はなかった。

　アリスは個人が所有する工場と同様に、陸海軍の軍需工場も調査したいと思った。陸軍はその製造や貯蔵所の調査を受け入れたが、海軍は調査するのを許可しなかったので、ついにアリスはワシントンの海軍の秘書官補との面会を申し入れたのだった。その若い秘書官補はアリスの話に注意深く耳を傾けていたが、それからひとりの高級将校を連れてきてくれた。そしてほどなく、海軍の工場調査の許可を得ることが出来たのだった。アリスは彼の迅速な対応に感謝したが、この若い秘書官補のフランクリン・ルーズベルトが、のちにアメリカ大統領になるなどとは夢にも思わな

かった。

　1917年4月、アメリカが第一次世界大戦に加わってからは、アリスはさらに多くの任務を求められるようになっていった。火薬工場は物資を製造するために、ほとんど夜通し稼動している状態だった。しかし、間もなくアリスは、数値では測ることのできない重大な変化に気づいた。それは、軍需工場で働く労働者の健康問題が、突然国家の関心事になったことだった。工場ではより多くの兵器を製造しなければならなかったので、従業員たちは健康である必要があった。その結果として、医師たちは労働者の厚生について真剣に考え始めた。そして、立法者たちと共に、アリスの仕事や彼女が以前から提案していた打開策について、話し合いを始めたのだった。

　終戦後、軍需工場で働く人々の健康への関心は、しだいに他の産業にも拡がっていった。今や産業医学は科学における最も重要視される分野の一つと認められ、アリス・ハミルトンは、しばしばその先駆者とされた。まだ調査すべき危険な職業は残っており、技術の進歩とともに新しい危険な作業が生まれていた。しかし、アリスの仕事は、けっして以前のように困難なものとはならないだろうと思われた。

　労働者の健康という新たな関心を反映して、ハーバード大学医学部では産業衛生部門が設立された。医師たちには、この新たなる分野の課題に対応するための訓練が必要であった。しかし、誰が彼らに教育できるのだろうか？　学部長はアリスがそれを引受けてくれることを望み、彼女を准教授として大学に迎えたいと申

し出た。もしアリスがそれを引受けるのなら、彼女はこの名門大学における最初の女性教員となるはずだった。

　しかしアリスは労働局の仕事を続けたいと思っており、また、学部長が提案していた百貨店を調査することには興味がなかったので、その返事を延ばして、予定していたアリゾナの銅鉱山の調査へ行くことにした。

　1919年1月のある寒い朝、アリスはこれまでの仕事の中で最高の冒険の一つとなる場所へ向かうため、ハルハウスを後にした。彼女はもう50歳になろうとしており、その表情や服装は初老を思わせた。そしてふと気がつくと、アリスはほとんどのおばあさんたちが真似したくはないと思っていることをやっていたのだった。

　アリゾナ州のグローブマイアミ鉱山地区では、アリスはスカートからオーバーオールに着替え、ランプ付のヘルメットを被った。そして「かご」という奇妙な名前のついている、四方に囲いのないエレベーターに勇ましく乗り込んだ。オールドドミニオン鉱山の底へ降りていくにつれ、かごが揺れたりしたが、掴まるものは何もなかった。地表から800フィートほど下がったところでエレベーターは停止した。

　ここからアリスの本当の冒険が始まった。鉱夫たちが削岩機で作業している現場を見るため、案内者に従いながら四つん這いになって斜面を登っていくと、彼らは銅を採掘するためにとても重い機械を使ってトンネルの壁に穴を開けていた。何人かの鉱夫たちは、この削岩機の強い振動が原因で健康を損ねているのだと報

告してきた。実際、次の日には、その鉱夫たちは吐き気を催し身体は衰弱していた。

　アリスは注意深く観察し、いくつかの削岩機だけに、岩石を湿らすため水の出るアタッチメントを取り付けていることに気がついた。そうすることによって、大量の粉塵を発生させることなく岩に穴を開けることが出来たのだった。鉱夫たちは、自分たちの身体を害しているのは削岩機の振動が原因だと思っていたので、粉塵についてアリスに不平を言うことはなかった。

　アリスは鉱山全体を調査した。そしてひとつの穴に入るために80フィートもの梯子を降りていって、高い手すりの上を這うようにして別の坑道へと移動していった。その手すりについている横木は手を伸ばさなければ届かないほど離れていたので、ひとつ間違えば奈落の底へ落ちてしまうようだった。アリスは自分を無理矢理落ち着かせながら、ゆっくりと注意深く案内者のあとについていった。

　暗闇から日の光の下に出てきた時、アリスは粉塵が削岩機の振動以上に鉱夫たちの健康に深刻な影響を与えていることを確信したので、他の鉱山に行った時に作業者や医師たちと話をして、湿式ドリルの使用の普及を強く勧めた。そして「自分でも削岩機を試してみて、それが実に使い心地の悪いものだと分かったけれど、その振動だけが永久的に身体の障害を引き起こす原因になるかどうかは分かりません」と説明した。

　以前にハーバード大学の学部長から提案されていた百貨店で働く従業員の健康調査は、アリゾナの鉱山で経験したものとは比較

のしようがないものだったので、家に帰る途中、アリスは失望感を覚えていた。その一方で彼女は、ハーバード大学で教鞭を取ることを望むようになっていた。それは新人医師たちに産業医学を教育指導するという、大きな満足感を彼女にもたらすと思われた。

　喜ばしいことに、ハルハウスで待ちかねていた彼女の元に、ハーバード大学から一通の手紙が届いた。大学は年半分の勤務という条件を申し入れてきたのだった。それで残りの６カ月を労働局の仕事に当てることが出来るし、また百貨店での調査をする必要もない。アリスは喜んで承諾の返事を書いた。

貢献しつづけること

　アリス・ハミルトンとジェーン・アダムスは、再び海を渡った。それはアリスがハーバード大学で仕事を始める以前の1919年4月の春のことだった。二人の女性は、戦争の及ぼす影響について議論する、スイスのチューリッヒで開催されている「第2回国際女性会議」へと向かった。

　会議では、ドイツ中で子供たちが餓死しているという衝撃的な話を耳にした。敗戦国が平和条件に同意するまで、戦勝国はドイツへの食料支援を停止していたからだった。この食料封鎖に、アリスは深い悲しみと怒りを覚えた。会議が終わったあと、アリスとジェーン・アダムスは、クエーカー教の米国友好奉仕委員会が食糧支援をしている貧困国を訪問した。

　そこで出会った子供たちは、青白く弱々しかった。フランクフルトの近くにある救済センターでは、学童たちが昼食を摂っていたが、みんな肋骨が数えられるほどやせ細っており、食べているものといえば、わずかな穀物の粒と切り刻んだ野菜の入ったほとんど水だけのスープだった。アリスはこの問題を取りあげて、母国の仲間たちに、いま目の当たりにしているこの子供たちの姿を見せることさえできれば、誰もが援助を厭わないだろうと信じていた。

　ボストンに戻って、アリスはハーバード大学で授業を始めたが、空いている時間はいつも、ドイツのクエーカー教の救済センターへの募金のための演説活動を行った。しかしすべての人が彼

女の取りあげているその問題に目を向けていたわけではなかった。多くの人たちは、まだドイツを敵とみなしていたので、「どうして善良なアメリカ人が自分の敵を助けようと思うのか」と彼らは反論した。

ついには大学関係者がやってきて、アリスにこの活動をやめるように言った。「ドイツ人の味方をする人のいる限り、誰もこの大学に寄付する人はいませんよ」と。それでは誰が飢えたドイツの子供たちのことを伝えるのでしょう？ アリスはそう思い、反対されながらも寄付を募り続けた。

また、工場を訪問することも止めなかった。1920年に労働局との契約を終えた時、彼女はハーバード大学の同僚たちとまだ調査を続けていた。フェルト帽製作工場に関する重要な調査では、そこで働く多くの従業員たちが大変奇妙な動作をするので、彼らは「頭のおかしくなった帽子屋」と呼ばれていた。これは作家のルイス・キャロルの書いた『不思議の国のアリス』の中で使われている滑稽な表現だった。しかし実際、毎日の作業で硝酸水銀塩の致死量の曝露を受けていれば、このような手足の震えや過敏な動作が引き起こされてもけっしておかしくはないと、アリスには分かっていた。

　　＊註：当時、帽子のフェルトの製造過程で使われる水銀が原因で水銀中毒の初期症状である手足の震えが現れていたため「帽子屋の震え」と呼ばれていた。

アリスは大学の同僚たちと、この健康を脅かすものについて、一般の人々の認識を向上させることに務めた。そして、水銀の使

用を徐々に法規制したので、フェルト帽製造業では、水銀化合物に代わって非中毒性の物質を使用せざるをえなくなった。

　フェルト帽製作工場と水銀採掘場での水銀中毒の調査は、アリスが初期に行っていた政府の調査で一酸化炭素とアニリン塗料を使用している工場の調査と同様に、いくつかの州で労働災害補償に関する法律の制定に役立った。これらの法の制定により、こういった仕事のために病気や怪我をしていた人々は、雇い主から経済的援助を受ける権利を得ることが出来るようになった。そして製造業者や保険会社は必要以上に余分なお金を支払いたくなかったので、安全で健康的な工場作りに励んだ。

　アリスは大学の授業とフィールド調査、その他の任務をほとんど休むことなく続けた。1924年から1930年の間は国際連盟保健機関の一員として働き、スイスのジュネーブでの最初の連盟委員会のあと、ソビエトの産業衛生を実際に調査するため同国へと旅立った。そして1925年、高い賞賛に値する産業医学に関する600ページにも及ぶ教科書*を出版した。

　＊註：Industrial Poisons in the United States

　1935年にハーバード大学を退職した後、アリスは妹のマーガレットや友人と一緒に暮らすため、コネチカット州のハドライムに帰った。このとき66歳だったが、アリスはエネルギッシュで何をすべきかについてよく分かっていた。そして、労働局の仕事を再開してビスコースレーヨンや人絹産業の研究を始めたが、この調査に基づいてペンシルバニア州議会で最初の労働災害補償の法律ができた。

貢献しつづけること 47

旅に出ていないときのアリスは、ハドライムの地域に住む人々との生活を楽しみ、この小さな町の行事に積極的に参加した。また園芸や友人とおしゃべりをするのが好きだった。アリスは自分のことを重要な有名人だとは少しも思っていなかった。

　ある日、エレノア・ルーズベルト夫人が、ハドライムの近くにあるコネチカット大学で演説をしたことがあった。彼女の夫のフランクリン・ルーズベルトが第一次大戦中、まだ秘書官補だった頃、自分を助けてくれた時の思い出をアリスは大切に胸にしまっていた。ルーズベルト夫人も人々のために献身していた女性だったので、アリスにとって彼女は尊敬に値する存在だった。

　同じ理由でルーズベルト夫人もまた、アリスを尊敬していた。彼女は演説をする前、「あなたも私と一緒に演壇に座って話してみませんか」とアリスを誘ったことがあったが、「とんでもありません」とアリスは慌てて答えた。「わたしは一人の観客にすぎませんわ」。そしてスポットライトを浴びることよりも、友人と目立たない客席にいるほうを選んだのだった。

　何年かのちに、そのとき一緒にいた友人はアリスについてこう語っている。「彼女は物事の中心になりたがるような人ではありませんでした。でも信じることがあればけっして臆することなく、その中心となって行動しているのです」と。

　「私は自分の生き方を少しも変えようとは思いませんでした」と、ある時アリスはこれまでの長い人生を振り返りながら言った。「新しくて広がりのある責務に参加することは、その人の一番良いものを引き出します。私にとっての満足は、今、物事がより

良くなっていって、それに何らかの役割を果たせたことです」。

　他の人たちも、アリスの成し遂げた重要な役割を心にとどめて忘れなかった。彼女には何年にも渡って、多くの賞と名誉が与えられた。1947年には、ニューイングランド年間最優秀女性医学者の称号を、そしてアメリカ公衆衛生局からは名誉あるラスカー賞が授与された。彼女の90歳の誕生日に祝意を表して、ハーバード大学の公衆衛生学部にアリス・ハミルトン基金が設立された。その２年後にはコネチカット大学の寄宿舎名が、アリスと、彼女の姉でのちに有名な作家となったエディス・ハミルトンの名前にちなんでつけられた。

　しかしアリスが思いもかけず、最も心を動かされたのは、退職してちょうど７年目に訪れた次の出来事ではないだろうか。アリスともう一人の客人がワシントンの労働局の職員食堂へ入った時、部屋にいた誰もが厳かに立ちあがった。そして、政府の職員たちがアリスのテーブルの前へきて、挨拶をしたのである。

　引退したあとでさえ、アリスは母の教えに導かれていた。いつでもやるべきことがあれば、彼女はそれをやり遂げる用意があった。アリスが最後に人々の前に姿を現わしたのは、アメリカのベトナム戦争への参戦に対する抗議の署名をした時であった。その時アリスは94歳。生きている限り、より良い世界を作りたいという彼女の決意は、揺るぎないものとなっていた。

あとがき

　1969年2月27日、アリス・ハミルトンはピンク色のナイトガウンを着てベッドの背にもたれていた。そして「平和と自由のための女性による国際連盟」の6人の代表者たちと挨拶をかわした。この日はアリスの100歳の誕生日で、国中の人々からの祝福の電話や花やカードが贈られた。ニクソン大統領からは、彼女の「世界中の人々の幸福のための止むことなき貢献」に対して感謝を綴った祝電が送られた。また何人かの友人たちはバースデーケーキを焼いてくれたが、それには6本のバラと1本の輝くろうそくが添えられてあった。

　晩年のアリスは多くのことに思いをめぐらしており、彼女が何を考えているのかを知ることは時には困難なこともあった。しかし誕生日を祝福されている時、ハルハウスで出会った貧しい子供たちのことやヨーロッパでの平和活動のこと、そして数え切れないほどの危険な工場を訪ねた時の懐かしい思い出が走馬燈のようにアリスの心に蘇っていたのかもしれない。

　それらの工場で出会った人たちも、今ではアリスと同じように年を取り、孫やひ孫はすでに仕事を持つほどの年齢に達しているだろう。そして彼らがどこで働いていようとも、新しい世代の人々は、アリスの残してきた研究の恩恵を受けているであろう。彼女は、労働者を護るために産業と医学が協力し合うという新しい流れを創り出した人であった。

　1970年9月、アリス・ハミルトンは101歳の生涯を終えた。そ

の年の12月には「自営業における保健基準を励行させる権利」を政府に与える連邦法が議会を通過した。

　アリスの献身と努力のおかげで、あらゆる職場で働く人々は皆同じように健康で、年を取っても生き生きとした人生を手に入れることができるだろう。

　ちょうどアリスがそうであったように。

訳者あとがき

　本書の翻訳は、産業医科大学医学部学生の平成10年の３年次教室配属実習の課題として、福島葉月君、浦本みほ君、邑本哲平君に課題の一つとして提示した本書の翻訳作業から始まりました。英語の力を養い、産業保健分野の歴史的課題を理解し、そしてこの分野の醍醐味を理解してもらうためです。学生諸君の個性の出た訳でしたが、これを機会に一冊の訳本として公にしてはと考え、吉村美穂氏とともに翻訳し直したものが本書です。

　学生諸君の思いのこもった原訳は、一般の人、小学校高学年あるいは中学生にもやさしく内容を伝える際の訳出に大変参考になりました。ここに謝意を表したいと思います。

　産業医学、産業保健の分野に対する理解を広め、さらにはこの分野を将来の職業として考える後進にロマンを感じとってもらうため、一人の人物の一生を平易に著した本書は、極めて適切と考えました。

　産業医科大学産業生態科学研究所環境疫学の高橋謙教授には、原書をお読み戴き、本書の日本語版作成の意義があるかを評価し、アドバイスを戴きました。産業医学振興財団の鹿毛明常務（当時）には、文章表現の手直しをして戴きました。また、改訂版では、山田剛彦氏に更新内容や読みやすくするためのアイデアなどをいただきました。ご尽力につきましてここに、御礼を申し上げます。なお、原書の出版者から、挿絵並びに英語原文の掲載のご許可を戴きました。ご理解に感謝します。最後に彼女の業績につ

いてまとめたプロフィールを年表とともに掲載しておきます。本書が産業保健・産業医学の分野の専門家のみならず、広くお読みいただけることを期待しております。

アリス・ハミルトン医学博士
Alice Hamilton, M.D.（1869.2.27-1970.9.22）

　米国において最初に産業医学の研究に生涯を捧げた女性医師。インディアナ州のフォートウェインの名門出で、経済的には堅実な家庭に生まれる。姉のエディス・ハミルトン（Edith Hamilton）は著名な古典学者である。1893年にミシガン大学医学部を卒業。

　1897年にノースウェスタン女子医科大学で教職についたのち、シカゴにあるジェーン・アダムス（Jane Addams）創立の厚生施設「ハルハウス」へ移り住んで、貧しい人々のために乳幼児診療所を開設する。この地域の住人たちと接しているうちに、かれらが奇妙な病による死に見舞われたり、鉛中毒や、手首下垂などに苦しんでおり、また多くの未亡人がいることを知った。ハルハウスの再建者たちの勧めで、これらの問題を医学知識によって解決する試みを始めた。ここに、職業関連疾患への取り組みが始まる。

　ハミルトン博士は、当時の米国において、職業性疾患についてほとんど記載されたものがなく、また理解もされていなかったことに気づいた。1908年に米国における職業性疾患についての最初の論文を発表したが、この後、この分野の権威者として認められることになる。そして1910年から、最初はイリノイ州の委員会の、後には連邦労働統計局の後援を受けて、職業性障害や社会的影響について調査を行った。

　この頃、主に「現場の疫学」に重点を置きながら、中毒学の実

験科学を起こし、米国の産業疫学と労働衛生の研究の草分けとなった。博士の研究は労働者の健康を改善するうえで大変科学的な説得力を持つものであったため、企業や社会の自主的な取組を促す原動力となり、さらには法制上の規制として活かされることになった。その典型例が、職業的鉛曝露の低減であった。

博士の最も専門とした調査研究は、鉄鋼業者の一酸化炭素中毒、帽子製造業者の水銀中毒、削岩機を使用する作業者に見られた白ろう病症候群などである。

調査研究の分野において、ハミルトン博士は科学的な誠実さを規範とし、また公衆衛生実務には慎重な技法を用いて、今日の産業保健の規範形成に影響を与えた。これには、問題に取り組むにあたっては、疾病の厳格な定義が必要であること、生産工程についての徹底的な理解がなければならないこと、そして、知見の速やかな報告と勧告を行うべきことが含まれる。

1919年、ハーバード大学医学部の産業衛生部門の准教授に任命された。彼女はハーバード大学の医学部における初めての女性の教授となった。このことは、米国における最も傑出した学問の府で、産業保健を立派な研究分野に位置づけたことを意味した。この間、国際連盟の健康委員会の委員を2期務め、66歳でハーバード大学を退職した後、米国労働局のコンサルタント業務の傍ら、米国消費者連盟の会長としても活躍した。

今日、オハイオ州シンシナティにある彼女の名前を冠した研究所やその他の施設で、米国疾病予防管理センター（CDC）の国立労働安全衛生研究所（NIOSH）に勤める研究者たちが今でも「危

険な職業」についての探求を続けている。

　アリス・ハミルトンは、医師であり、科学者であり、人道主義者であった。そして、20世紀における米国の社会改革運動における異論の余地のない指導者であった。

活動年表

1869年　米国ニューヨーク市で生誕後、インディアナ州フォートウェインで育つ。

1893年　ミシガン大学医学部で医学博士学位を取得後、女性と子供のためのミネアポリスのノースウェスタン病院およびニューイングランド病院でインターンシップを修了。

1895年～1897年　ドイツのミュンヘン大学およびライプチヒ大学にて細菌学と病理学を専攻、帰国後ジョンズ・ホプキンス大学医学部大学院にて研究を続ける。

1897年　シカゴへ移り、ノースウェスタン女子医科大学の病理学教授となり、その後、ジェーン・アダムスが創立したハルハウス[*1]のメンバーの一員となる。

1908年　イリノイ州の職業病委員会（Occupational Diseases Commission）の委員に就任。

1919年　ハーバード大学医学部産業衛生(Industrial Medicine)部門の初の女性准教授として採用される。

1924～1930年　国際連盟保健機関（League of Nations Health Committee）の唯一の女性委員として貢献。

1925年　Industrial Poisons in the United States出版。

1934年　Industrial Toxicology出版。

1935年　ハーバード大学退職後は名誉教授の肩書きを持ち、米国Div. of Labor Standardsの医療コンサルタントと

	して奉仕。
1943年	自伝Exploring the Dangerous Tradesを出版。
1944年	Men in Scienceのリストに加えられる。
1944〜1949年	全米消費者連盟（National Consumers League）[*2] 代表として貢献。
1947年	ラスカー賞（Lasker Award）[*3]受賞。
1970年	101歳の生涯を終える。
1973年	没後、米国National Women's Hall of Fame[*4] に任命される。
1987年	アリス・ハミルトン労働安全衛生研究所（Alice Hamilton Laboratory for Occupational Safety and Health）[*5] が設立。
1995年	55セント記念切手にハミルトンの肖像画が描かれる。
2002年	産業医学発展の貢献を評価するものとしてNational Historic Chemical Landmark[*6] を表彰される。

＊註：

＊1 ハルハウス：1889年、米国のソーシャルワークの先駆者ジェーン・アダムス（のちのノーベル平和賞受賞者）が友人のエレン・ゲイツ・スターとの共同で、近在の貧しい労働階級者のために設立した当時世界最大規模の福祉施設。

＊2 全米消費者連盟（National Consumers League）：1891年設立。1899年にジェーン・アダムスとジョセフィン・ローウェルにより認可される。

＊3 ラスカー賞（Lasker Award）：1946年 アルバート・ラスカー夫

妻によって始められた医学において主要な貢献をした人に与えられる米国医学会最高の賞。
*4 National Women's Hall of fame：1969年にニューヨークに設立された建物で様々な分野で社会貢献をした優れたアメリカ人女性の栄誉を讃え、その功績が展示されている。1848年「女性の権利のための会議」が最初に開かれた場所でもある。
*5 アリスハミルトン労働安全衛生研究所（Alice Hamilton Laboratory for Occupational Safety and Health）：米国国立労働安全衛生研究所（NIOSH）により設立。優秀な研究者にはアリス・ハミルトン賞（Alice HamiltonAward）を授与している。
*6 National Historic Chemical Landmark：1992年米国化学協会により設立された化学の功績に偉業を成し遂げた研究者として表彰される。

代表的伝記等

【成　書】

1　Grant, Madeleine P. Alice Hamilton：Pioneer Doctor in Industrial Medicine.New York：Abelard-Schuman, 1967
2　Hamilton, Alice. Exploring the Dangerous Trades：The Autobiography of Alice Hamilton.
　　Boston：Little, Brown, and Company, 1943
3　Sicherman, Barbara. Alice Hamilton：A Life in Letters. Cambridge：Harvard University Press, 1984

【論　文】

4　Felton, JeanSpencer, M.D. "Industrial Health as a Specialty：A Medical Field of Interest to Women's Physicians", Journal of the American Medical Women's Association（June 1947）：294-299
5　Hamilton, Alice. "Pioneering in Industrial Medicine", Journal of the American Medical Women's Association（June 1947）：292-293
6　Hamilton, Alice. "A Woman of Ninety Looks at Her World". The Atlantic（September 1961）：51-55
7　"Edith and Alice Hamilton：Students in Germany", The Atlantic（March 1965）：129-132

8 "Nineteen Years in the Poisonous Trades", "Harper's (October 1929) : 580-591

9 Hardy, Harriet L.,ed.Journal of Occupational Medicine (February 1972). Special issue dedicated to Alice Hamilton.

10 Sergeant, ElizabethShepley, "Alice Hamilton,M.D. : Crusader for Health in Industry", Harper's (May 1926) : 763-770

11 Urbano,Judy, "Doctor's Life Spanned Hull House, Labor Strife" and "Pioneering Doctor Made Hadlyme Her Last Home". Parts I, II. TheGazette, October 26 and November 2, 1978. (Courtesy of the Lyme Public Library Lyme, Connecticut)

12 "Dr.Alice Hamilton Celebrates 100th Birthday : Famed Industrial Toxicologist is Honored for her Work in Mines and Factories", Special to The New York Times, February 29, 1969

The Workers' Detective

The Workers' Detective

A Story about Dr. Alice Hamilton

by Stephanie
Sammartino McPherson
illustrations by Janet Schulz

A Carolrhoda Creative Minds Book

Carolrhoda Books, Inc./Minneapolis

To my husband, Dick, with thanks for his support and encouragement

Special thanks to the Fort Wayne and Allen County Public Libraries, Indiana; Connecticut College Archives; and the Lyme Public Library, Lyme, Connecticut

Copyright © 1992 by Stephanie Sammartino McPherson
Illustrations copyright © 1992 by Carolrhoda Books, Inc.
All rights reserved. International copyright secured. No part of this book may be reproduced, stored in a retrieval system, or transmitted in any form or by any means, electronic, mechanical, photocopying, recording, or otherwise, without the prior written permission of the Publisher except for the inclusion of brief quotations in an acknowledged review.

Library of Congress Cataloging-in-Publication Data

McPherson, Stephanie Sammartino.
   The workers' detective : a story about Dr. Alice Hamilton / by Stephanie Sammartino McPherson ; illustrated by Janet Schulz.
      p. cm. — (A Creative minds book)
   Includes bibliographical references.
   Summary: A biography of Dr. Alice Hamilton, social worker and doctor, whose work brought attention to the health risks associated with particular jobs.
   ISBN 0-87614-699-X (lib. bdg.)
   1. Hamilton, Alice, 1869-1970—Juvenile literature. 2. Industrial hygienists—United States—Biography—Juvenile literature. [1. Hamilton, Alice, 1869-1970. 2. Industrial hygienists. 3. Physicians. 4. Social workers.] I. Schulz, Janet, ill. II. Title. III. Series: Creative minds (Minneapolis, Minn.)
RC964.34.H35M36 1992
616.9'803'092—dc20
[B]   91-23634
                                                        CIP
                                                         AC

Manufactured in the United States of America
2 3 4 5 6 7 – P/MA – 00 99 98 97 96

Table of Contents

Introduction	6
Two Kinds of People	9
Thirst for Adventure	17
Medical Mystery	26
Blazing the Trail in Industrial Medicine	37
Dangers Above and Below	45
Lasting Contributions	53
Afterword	61
Select Bibliography	63

Introduction

When Alice Hamilton was born in February 1869, industry in the United States had entered a new period of growth. Ever since the Civil War had ended, the nation had been concentrating its energies on building steamships and extending railroad and telegraph lines. New inventions improved methods of manufacturing chemicals, steel, and machinery. Electricity provided a powerful new energy source. Soon factories were producing more goods and shipping them more easily than ever before.

Other changes were also taking place. As growing factories hired more people, cities grew, too. Industry spread from New England and the East Coast to the rest of the country. Progress was so rapid and exciting that this time of change became known as the Industrial Revolution in both the United States and Europe.

Unfortunately, few Americans thought to wonder

about the possible dangers of these developments. People were too fascinated by the new variety and quantity of goods available to worry about the workers who made them. But Alice Hamilton changed all that.

① Two Kinds of People

Gathering up[*1] her skirt with one hand and waving a wooden sword with the other, young Alice Hamilton chased her cousins in and out of the apple orchard. Clash! Bang! went their make-believe weapons as King Arthur and the Knights of the Round Table triumphed over[*2] their foes.

No matter how often they acted the scene, the children always had fun. Sometimes they pretended the apple orchard was Sherwood Forest, and they became Robin Hood and his band of merry men. Other times they brought the legend of the Trojan horse to life.

Whatever the children played, there were always plenty of actors to bring the drama to life. The four Hamilton girls — Edith, Alice, Margaret, and Norah — lived only a field away from one set of lively cousins. Other cousins who lived nearby came almost every day to join in the games. Alice and her cousins Agnes and Allen were so close in

---

*1　Gathering up　（スカートなどを）たくしあげる
*2　triumph over　打ち負かす、勝利を得る

age and spent so much time together that they were nicknamed "the three A's."

Merrily the three A's and their companions trooped in and out of*³ Alice's house, Agnes's house, and Grandmother Hamilton's house, which were all located on the same property in Fort Wayne, Indiana. Called Old House, Grandmother Hamilton's home was very large and grand. Her husband, a successful businessman and one of the founders of Fort Wayne, had left his family financially secure.

Grandmother Hamilton was a strong supporter of women's rights. Someday, she predicted, women would have the same kinds of jobs as men. Someday they would be given the right to own property and vote. Through her involvement in the women's rights movement, Mrs. Hamilton became a good friend of Susan B. Anthony. The famous suffragist had devoted herself to winning women the right to vote. She had an open invitation to stay at Old House whenever she passed through*⁴ Indiana.

Like Grandmother Hamilton, Alice's mother was also an independent woman for her time. She encouraged her daughters to speak up*⁵ about their beliefs. "There are two kinds of people," Gertrude Hamilton declared, "the ones who say, 'Somebody

---

*3　in and out of　出たり入ったりして
*4　pass through　通り過ぎる
*5　speak up　はっきりと言う

ought to do something about it, but why should it be I?' and those who say, 'Somebody must do something about it, then why not I?'"

"Two kinds of people." Alice never forgot the words. Even as a young girl, she knew which kind of person she wanted to be. She hoped she would do something important, something to help people and to make the world a better place.

But what would that be? This was a hard question for a girl who knew little of the world beyond the Hamilton family. Except for her cousins, Alice did not even know other children in Fort Wayne because Gertrude and Montgomery Hamilton taught their children at home. Alice and her sisters learned Latin from their father, French from their mother, and German from the servants. The girls studied history, religion, and literature, too.

Even Alice's vacations were different from those of less privileged children. Summertime meant going to a vacation spot on Mackinac Island that the Hamilton family had visited every summer since 1879, when Alice was ten years old. The island was located in the straits between Lake Huron and Lake Michigan. Each year as the boat neared the shore, Alice strained to[*6] catch glimpses

---

*6　strain to　〜しようと努める
　　例）She strained to hear the sound.
　　　　彼女はその音に一生懸命耳をすました。

11

of familiar landmarks. She wanted to make sure[*7] nothing had changed in the woods, the pine cliffs, and the pebbled beaches.

Alice enjoyed her carefree childhood, both on Mackinac Island and in Fort Wayne. But as she grew up, some things began to change. She was fourteen when Allen's parents sent him to school in Boston. In Allen's letters to Alice, he included descriptions of his science studies, especially physics. How fascinating it sounded! Eagerly she told her father that she would like to learn physics, too. Mr. Hamilton, a banker and wholesale grocer, had little interest in science himself. "It is all in the encyclopedia," he said. And he was right. The only problem was that Alice could scarcely understand a word of the long, technical account.

A year later, Alice read a book that was much more interesting. It started her thinking about a different branch of science—medicine. *The Merv Oasis* was a detailed travel diary of a diplomat's journey to Persia. Alice imagined herself in the distant land, finding adventure wherever she went. She thought of the people she might meet. Some would be sick, some would be poor. She dreamed of becoming a medical missionary and caring for these people who had no one else to help them.

---

*7　make sure　確かめる

12

Alice had many dreams, however, and was not yet ready to study medicine. Two years later, in 1886, her parents sent her to a girls' boarding school in Connecticut, where she studied languages and philosophy. What she learned from her classmates, though, was almost more important than what she learned from her classes. During the required daily walks, Alice had long talks with the other girls. Most of her new friends had attended other schools before this one. They knew more people and had a broader range of experiences than she did. Alice began to realize what an unusual childhood she had led.

By the time Alice returned to Fort Wayne, she had become a determined young woman eager to face the world. She was also eager to[*8] see her family, which had grown to include a two-year-old brother, Arthur. By now Alice was old enough to be thinking about marrying and having children of her own. But she was much more interested in a career than in romance. I want to be a doctor, she confided to[*9] her sister Edith during one of their many talks about the future.

Like Alice, Edith wanted a career of her own. But Edith was shocked at her sister's unconventional choice. Alice's parents were worried about

---

*8 eager to 〜したいと熱望する
*9 confide to 打ち明ける

her decision, too. Many people still considered medicine an unsuitable profession for the "gentle sex," even though forty years had passed since Elizabeth Blackwell had become the first female doctor in the United States. In the years since Dr. Blackwell had made history, about forty-five hundred women had received medical degrees. But female physicians did not have nearly the number of opportunities that men did.

Alice had made her decision carefully, though, and would not be turned from her goal. "As a doctor, I could go anywhere I please," she said, "to far-off lands or city slums—and be quite sure I could be of use anywhere. I should meet all sorts and conditions of men, [and] I should not be tied down[*10] to a school or college as a teacher is or have to work under a superior as a nurse must do."

Alice set out[*11] to teach herself the sciences she would need to enter medical school. Her dedication and hard work convinced her parents that she had a future as a doctor after all. By 1890 twenty-one-year-old Alice had learned enough on her own and through a small, local school to be accepted at the University of Michigan, one of the top-ranked medical schools in the country. She was one of only thirteen women in her class.

---

*10 tie down （人・物を）〜で縛って押さえておく、拘束する
*11 set out 〜し始める

15

② Thirst for Adventure

 Peering through a microscope, Alice concentrated on*¹² pink- and blue-stained cells. All around her, other young men and women were bent over microscopes, too. There were never quite enough microscopes to go around,*¹³ so Alice was glad she had arrived at class early enough to claim one. Nothing fascinated her more than viewing the cell, the basic structure of life, through the magnifying lens. In her histology class, she learned to recognize healthy cells, and in pathology class, she examined samples of diseased cells. A hardworking student, she didn't want to miss a thing.
 By the time Alice received her medical degree in

---

*12 concentrate on 集中する
*13 enough …go around 十分に〜が皆に行きわたる
   例）There are not enough foods to go around.
    食糧は十分に行きわたっていない。

1893, she had decided to devote her life to research in pathology. She wanted to study the causes of disease at the most basic level. She knew that when people became sick, some of their cells were affected. What caused these normal cells to change and even die? And how did these changes cause the symptoms of certain illnesses? These were the kinds of questions Alice hoped to answer by examining cells in a laboratory. But first she had to complete an internship. This would give her practical experience with patients and help her find a permanent job once she graduated.

That summer Alice had to leave Mackinac Island early to begin her training. Watching the island grow smaller as her father steered the boat toward*14 the mainland, she felt homesick already. What would her year as an intern be like? she wondered. Would she be able to handle the patients properly?

As soon as she began her duties, Alice was overworked. Her internship was at Northwestern Hospital, a facility for women and children in Minneapolis. She was expected to diagnose illnesses, mix medicines, and deliver babies all by herself. The unscientific methods of the senior doctors did not make her job easier. In a letter to

---

*14　steer … toward　〜に向けて舵を取る

her cousin Agnes, Alice explained her dismay. "All the accurately careful, elaborate work that I have been taught to consider so important is ignored here, and I am expected to make off-hand diagnoses, rapid prescriptions, and meet emergencies without losing my head. None of which I can do at all. There is no laboratory [and] the microscope is not as good as my own."

Alice soon realized she could help patients in spite of*15 these handicaps. But two months later, she was offered another internship in Boston, and she decided to leave Northwestern Hospital. She was lonely in Minneapolis, and the New England Hospital had a fine reputation. Like Northwestern, this was a facility for women and children. (In those days, it was considered improper for female doctors to have men for patients.)

Upon her arrival in Boston, Alice was assigned to*16 the maternity ward. Although she helped deliver many healthy babies, sometimes there was nothing she could do to save an infant or lessen a mother's pain. When one new mother died, Alice could hardly control her grief. The woman had been young and gentle, with much to live for. Alice realized that she was indeed better suited for work in a laboratory than as a practicing doctor. The

---

*15 in spite of ～にもかかわらず
*16 be assigned to ～に任命される、割り当てられる

19

stress and emotional involvement of patient care was too overwhelming for her.

After several months, Alice was transferred to[*17] the dispensary, or home-care clinic. This new position required her to make house calls. Alice never knew where her job would take her—to dingy basements, narrow attics, or tiny rooms over saloons. All over the Boston slums she traveled on foot, sometimes not returning home until after midnight.

On her medical rounds, Alice met many immigrants who could not find work. Often she visited families who were hungry or in need of clothing or coal to heat their homes. Alice put these families in touch with[*18] local charities that could help them. In a small but important way, she was beginning to make a difference in the world.

Another intern, named Rachelle Slobodinsky, was also determined to make a difference. Russian by birth,[*19] Rachelle had fled her native land at the age of seventeen. When she had arrived in New York, she had taken a job in a sweatshop, a small factory where employees were required to work long hours in hot, dirty rooms. The workers received little pay for their labors. Alice listened to the story of Rachelle's life with fascination

---

*17　be transferred to　〜へ転任する、移動する
*18　put … in touch with　〜を〜に紹介する
　　　例）She put me in touch with her sister.
　　　　　彼女は自分の妹を紹介してくれた。
*19　by birth　〜生まれ

20

and dismay. "Tell me everything," she urged her new friend.

For the first time, Alice felt ashamed of her easy, carefree upbringing. While Alice had been enjoying herself at a private school, Rachelle had been working for a living. "She is only our age, but she has lived through more than we will have when we are sixty," Alice wrote to Agnes.

Alice completed her internship in 1894. She still did not want to be a practicing physician, but she did want to help people who faced hardships like Rachelle's. Somehow she hoped to combine pathology with social work. However, her professors advised her to first study in Germany, which was considered the center for advanced training in pathology. This prospect especially appealed to Alice because her sister Edith, a graduate in literature from Pennsylvania's Bryn Mawr College, was also planning to study in Germany. By 1895 both sisters had returned to Fort Wayne to prepare for the trip.

One day Alice and Edith were busy with their travel plans when their youngest sister, Norah, came bursting into the room. Excitedly, Norah announced that Jane Addams, the famous social worker, was to speak in Fort Wayne that very evening.

---

*20 ashamed of 恥じている
*21 live through 生き抜く、切り抜ける
*22 combine … with ～を～と結び付ける、組合わせる
*23 burst into ～に飛び込むように入ってくる

Jane Addams! To think that the founder of Hull House would actually be coming through their town! Alice had never seen the poor Chicago neighborhood where Miss Addams had opened her settlement house and offered food, shelter, and other services to those in need. But Alice had read all about the famous social experiment. She knew that Miss Addams and the other resident volunteers at Hull House were always ready to receive their neighbors, usually poor immigrant workers and their families.

That night Alice, Norah, and Agnes attended Jane Addams's speech. Fascinated by everything she heard, Alice realized that she and Miss Addams shared the same goals. Suddenly she knew she had found the perfect way to combine laboratory research and social work. She would become a pathologist, but she would spend her evenings and weekends working in a settlement house.

Shortly after hearing Miss Addams speak, Alice left with Edith for Germany, where they studied first in Leipzig and later in Munich. Although she enjoyed making German friends, Alice did not learn much pathology that she had not already known. In class women were officially "invisible." In order to[*24] attend one special lecture,

---

*24　in order to　～するために

Alice had to be escorted by an elderly physician to a chair in the corner of the room before the other doctors entered. And wherever she went, the same question seemed to follow her: "If American women go into[*25] science, who will darn the stockings?"

When she returned to the United States, Alice could not find a job, so she continued her study of pathology at Johns Hopkins University, in Baltimore. A year later, in 1897, she accepted a position as a professor at the Women's Medical College of Northwestern University, in Chicago. Right away Alice knew where she wanted to live!

Nervous but hopeful, Alice went to Hull House to speak with Miss Addams. Just as Alice had imagined, Miss Addams was sympathetic and kind. But she did not have good news. All the rooms at Hull House were occupied by other volunteers. There was no room for another resident.

Alice did not pause to[*26] rest. She marched several miles north to another settlement house called the Commons. Once more she was turned away. Tired and disappointed, Alice wondered how she would achieve her goal of combining science and social work.

That summer Alice turned to the quiet beauty

---

*25　go into　（職業など）に入る、従事する、つく
*26　pause to　立ち止まって〜する

of Mackinac Island for comfort. She knew that medical work alone could not satisfy her thirst for adventure. Never had she felt so uncertain about her future. Then one morning the mail boat brought her a letter from Jane Addams. Alice was thrilled to*27 learn that a room at Hull House would be available*28 after all. The young doctor could begin her life at the settlement house that October.

---

*27　thrill to　〜に胸躍る、わくわくする
*28　be available　使用可能になる、空く
　　　例）The hotel have no available rooms.
　　　　そのホテルには空き部屋はない。

25

③
Medical Mystery

In many ways, Hull House, with its elegant design and high ceilings, reminded Alice of Old House.*29 But her life in the lovely old settlement house was nothing like*30 her sheltered childhood. Although Alice had seen poverty in Boston, in Chicago she lived in the middle of it.

The men and women who visited Hull House worked long hours in factories for very little money. Their homes were small, stuffy rooms in crowded

---

*29 remind … of　～に～を思い出させる
　　例）That story reminded me of a joke.
　　　　その話はあるジョークを思い出させた。

*30 nothing like…　～とは別物である、ほど遠い

tenement apartments. Rats scampered through the alleys around these buildings, and smelly garbage overflowed its containers.

Because her patients were also her neighbors, she developed an even stronger understanding of their hopes and hardships than she had developed with her patients in Boston.

Anxious to[*31] help everyone, Alice made house calls to sick children and founded a well-baby clinic where mothers could bring their young children for checkups and baths. She tried to teach people how to prevent illnesses, though often this was difficult. The women did not understand how bacteria spread, and at thirty years old, Alice looked too young to be an expert. But her gentle smile and friendly concern appealed to parents as well as their children.

Besides caring for her neighbors' health, Alice wanted to enrich their lives with beauty and learning. Enthusiastically she taught art and English classes at night. She also helped with the boys' club and supervised the men's athletic club. On weekends she liked to take children for picnics in the country. The grateful youngsters often followed her noisily as she bustled down the streets near Hull House. How she longed to[*32] help

---

*31　anxious to　〜を切望する
*32　long to　〜することを強く願う、切望する

27

these boys and girls find a better life!

Sometimes Alice picketed with the children's parents when they went on strike for higher wages and shorter working hours. Risking arrest, she held her sign high and marched back and forth*33 in front of the factories.

When Alice had been at Hull House five years, the women's medical school where she taught became part of the men's school. The new coeducational school did not have a position for Alice. So she found a new job as a bacteriologist at the Memorial Institute for Infectious Diseases. But Alice's life at Hull House was more absorbing than her life in the laboratory.

The more Alice got to know the factory workers at Hull House, the more*34 they told her about their illnesses and physical disabilities. An alarming pattern began to emerge as Alice listened to the tales of her neighbors. Pale, thin, and prematurely wrinkled, the painters and lead-factory workers suffered from*35 indigestion and sometimes had trouble moving their wrists and hands properly—all symptoms of lead poisoning. Workers in steel mills told of breathing carbon monoxide, while those employed in the stockyards seemed to have high rates of pneumonia and rheumatism.

---

*33　back and forth　行きつ戻りつ、前後に、あちこちに
*34　the more… the more　〜すればするほど〜する
*35　suffer from　〜に悩まされる、苦しむ

Some people claimed fatigue was responsible for[*36] these problems, but Alice suspected that poor conditions in the factories were ruining the workers' health.

In 1907 Alice discovered a book by Thomas Oliver that confirmed her suspicions. It was called *Dangerous Trades*, and it was all about the health risks of certain jobs. Thomas Oliver had done a fine job of surveying the British industrial scene. After finishing the volume, Alice decided to see what had been written about American factories.

To her amazement, Alice could not find any literature on the subject. She turned to other doctors for help, and here, too, she was in for a surprise. American workers did not suffer from industrial poisons, her colleagues declared.

Alice had lived too long at Hull House to accept these easy answers. All around her, Americans were suffering dreadful disabilities and sometimes *dying*—simply from doing their jobs!

Something had to be done, she realized. Someone had to prove what was happening in American factories. Although laws had been passed in several states in an attempt to[*37] protect workers' health, little had been achieved. Alice felt she was striking out in a brand-new field.

---

*36　responsible for　〜が原因である
*37　attempt to　〜を試みる、企てる

Alice continued to talk to workers. She investigated every clue about their mysterious illnesses. In September 1908, she published her first article on the subject, encouraging Americans to rally for better working conditions. She also addressed the issue of women's health. Women who worked with lead suffered even more severe disorders than men who worked with lead, she believed. Women often worked in warm, damp surroundings such as laundries or canning factories. These conditions increased the risk of heart disease and tuberculosis and caused some pregnant women to lose their babies. Soon many people knew of Alice's interest, but few people were able to supply her with*38 proof of her theories.

Finally, when Alice was thirty-nine years old, a visitor named John Andrews came to Hull House with important evidence to show her. He had done a study of a strange illness called phossy jaw. The terrible disease caused facial bones to slip out of place and the jaw to swell up*39 painfully. In severe cases, patients lost an eye or a jawbone. Only one group of people ran the risk of*40 phossy jaw—workers in match factories. Their illness had been linked to*41 the phosphorus they breathed while performing their jobs.

---

*38 supply … with 〜に〜を与える、供給する、提供する
*39 swell up 腫れ上がる
*40 run the risk of 〜の危険に身をさらしている
*41 link to 〜と連携している、関連している

Eagerly Alice pored over[*42] the report. She knew all about phossy jaw, but other medical experts claimed the disease was unknown in the United States. Here was proof they were wrong. John Andrews had discovered more than 150 cases of phossy jaw among American match workers! Alice could use this information to educate others and to stir up[*43] interest within the medical community.

Within two years of the report's publication, a new law banned the use of phosphorus in match making. Rapidly, a new substance called sesqui-sulphide was substituted for[*44] phosphorus. Soon phossy jaw was a disease of the past.

The work of Alice Hamilton, John Andrews, and other observant people was slowly bringing change to American industry. In December 1908, the governor of Illinois created an Occupational Disease Committee. Already considered an expert in the field, Alice was asked to join the nine-member panel. And since Alice knew more about industrial medicine than anyone else on the committee, she was asked to be the managing director of the survey. Together the experts would study industrial hygiene, or cleanliness, in Illinois factories and make a list of dangerous jobs.

Alice felt challenged and determined. But she

---

*42　pore over　熟読する
*43　stir up　かきたてる
*44　be substituted for　〜の代用になる

was overwhelmed at the same time. No one knew all the occupational hazards facing the workers of Illinois. Alice could only hope to discover them as she went along.*45

Taking time away from the laboratory, Alice got right to work. Her special topic in the survey was lead poisoning, a much bigger field than she had first imagined. Touring factories all around the state, she interviewed workers in trades known to expose their workers to lead.

What is the hardest part of your job?

How long have you worked here?

Are you as healthy now as you were when you began this job?

These were the kinds of questions Alice asked the surprised workers. No one had ever taken an interest in their lives like this. Some men were afraid of losing their jobs if they spoke with Alice. Others, responding to her warmth and concern, told her what she needed to know about their jobs and their health.

But Alice wanted a broader picture than her factory visits could give her. She spent hours reading patient histories in hospitals all over the state. When she discovered cases of lead poisoning, she went to see the victims in their homes.

---

*45　as…go along　（人が）やっていく、続けていく、進んでいく

33

She spoke with their families. Many of them were immigrants, alone and bewildered in this new country. Alice let them know that she cared what happened to them.

On one visit, Alice was puzzled*46 by a man with severe stomach pain and trembling hands. From his hospital records, she was certain the man had lead poisoning. But she did not know why. He told Alice that he put enamel on bathtubs—not a job she associated with*47 high exposure to lead. So Alice set out to*48 investigate. She found workers sprinkling ground enamel over tubs that were hot enough to melt the fine, white powder. The air was heavy with enamel dust. The workers could not help but*49 breathe it in.

When Alice explained what she was doing, one of them gave her a sample of the powder to take home. Her detective work paid off.*50 She tested the powder in the laboratory and was shocked to learn the enamel was twenty percent lead. Even the more advanced Europeans had failed to note this. No longer was the man's illness a mystery. Grimly Alice added enameling to her list of dangerous trades.

No one involved in the survey expected Alice to do anything about the conditions she found—

---

*46　be puzzled　〜に戸惑う、困惑する
*47　associate with　〜を連想する、関連づける
*48　set out to　〜に着手する、し始める
*49　cannot help but…　〜せずにいられない、避けられない
*50　pay off　（物事が）うまくいく

35

except to report them. But how many people would suffer health problems before changes were made? Someone had to speak for them now. Alice still remembered her mother's long-ago words. "Two kinds of people," Gertrude Hamilton had said. Alice realized that reporting what she had seen was not enough.

Although it was not part of her job, Alice tried to convince employers to improve working conditions. One day she spoke with Edward Cornish, vice president of the National Lead Works, a company that owned several factories in Chicago. Bravely she told him his men were being poisoned.

At first Mr. Cornish was angry at her accusations. But Alice was so kind and sincere in spite of her charges that he stopped to think. "I don't believe you are right," he said at last, "but I can see you do." And he told Alice that if she could show that his workers were being poisoned, he would do everything she asked.

Rising to the challenge, Alice proved her detective skills by discovering twenty-two cases of lead poisoning among his workers. Mr. Cornish was surprised and impressed. He kept his promise to Alice and reformed his factories.

④
Blazing the Trail in Industrial Medicine

Like a real detective, Alice followed every clue as she worked to establish the relationships between workers' illnesses and their jobs. "This industrial diseases work is like trying to make one's way[*51] through a jungle and not even being able to find an opening," she wrote in 1910. But Alice made her own openings. Before the committee submitted its report in January 1911, Alice had discovered seventy-seven lead-related trades and documented more than five hundred cases of lead poisoning.

Responding to the hard evidence the committee had uncovered, the Illinois legislature passed an occupational disease law in 1911. Now employers were required to follow safety precautions and provide monthly checkups for workers who handled certain dangerous substances. Six other states also passed occupational-disease laws that year. This was tremendous progress, but Alice knew

---

＊51　make one's way　（苦労して）進む

there was much more to do. If only the American medical profession would take a greater interest in industry, her job would be much easier.

The members of the committee knew this, too. They decided to send Alice to the International Congress on Occupational Accidents and Diseases in Brussels, Belgium, to learn about advances in the field. Although this was a wonderful opportunity, it meant Alice had even less time for her laboratory work. But she believed she could make greater contributions to the new field of industrial medicine than to pathology. Eagerly she set off[*52] for the conference.

In Brussels Alice heard noted European experts speak on all aspects of industrial medicine. Alice spoke, too. She presented a paper about white lead, a substance containing lead that was used in some paints. The European doctors were very interested in her comments. What is the rate of lead poisoning in different jobs? they asked her. What are your laws for regulating the dangerous trades?

To Alice's disgrace, she had no answers to their questions. Finally a Belgian doctor ended the discussion, saying, "It is well known that[*53] there is no industrial hygiene in the United States."

---

*52　set off　出発する
*53　It is well known that…　〜についてはよく分かる、よく知られている

Alice felt her face grow hot with embarrassment.

Charles O'Neill was also embarrassed. He was the U.S. Commissioner of Labor and one of the few other Americans at the conference. Shortly after Alice returned to the United States, Mr. O'Neill sent her a letter asking for a very big commitment. Would Alice do for the entire nation what she was doing for Illinois?

At forty-two years old, Alice had reached a crossroads in her life. If she accepted the new position, she did not know when she would get back to laboratory work. She also knew that as a federal investigator, she would have many responsibilities and few privileges. On her own, she would have to identify and locate factories. She would have to convince the owners to let her inside and make her own guidelines for how to proceed. And she would not get paid until each report was finished.

These seemed like hard terms, but industrial medicine meant too much to Alice for her to pass up*54 such an exciting opportunity. She accepted the position in Washington, D.C., and never returned to research again. She did, however, continue to spend time at Hull House. Although Alice's new job took her all over the East and

---

*54　pass up　断る、見送る

40

Midwest, she still considered the settlement her home and spent as much time there as possible. It was always good to return to friends who understood her commitment and enthusiasm.

For her first national survey, Alice again chose lead and set about*55 locating and visiting factories. Some foremen in these factories must have bristled at the thought of allowing a stranger to come in and criticize their management—and it must not have helped that she was a woman. But Alice would explain that she was there to help them, not to stir up resentment with the workers. Happy, healthy employees made for a better-running factory, she would point out.*56 Alice's quiet sincerity and unfailing courtesy convinced the owners that she was their friend. Factory after factory opened its doors for her inspection.

And factory after factory failed to*57 meet the most basic health standards. Everywhere she went, Alice found men eating their lunches with lead-encrusted hands, men whose hair was plastered with*58 lead. Worst of all, she found men breathing in the dangerous lead dust and fumes.

Sometimes the conditions she found made her angry, but she stayed calm.*59 In spite of everything she saw, Alice believed that factory owners cared

---

*55　set about　〜に取りかかる
*56　point out　指摘する
*57　faile to　(〜しようとして) できない、し損ねる
*58　be plastered with　〜がべたべたとくっついている
*59　stay calm　冷静を保つ、平静さを保つ

about their employees just as Mr. Cornish did. So after she inspected a factory, she would convince the owners and managers to make important changes. She told them how to use fans and vents to pull fresh air into the workrooms and minimize the dust. She encouraged them to provide regular medical checkups for all employees.

Although men still dominated the medical profession, Alice felt that being a woman helped her achieve reforms in industrial hygiene. "Employers and doctors both appeared more willing to listen to me as I told them their duties than they would have been if I had been a man," she wrote years later. "It seemed natural and right that a woman should put care of the producing workman ahead of the value of the thing he was producing."

After five years of studying lead, Alice began to investigate the rubber industry. But other issues were claiming her attention, too. Europe was fighting the Great War, World War I. Alice, who labored ceaselessly for the lives of people on the job, was horrified at*60 the thought of young men losing their lives on the battlefield.

Jane Addams shared Alice's desire for a peaceful Europe. In 1915 the famous social worker decided to attend the International Congress of

---

*60　be horrified at　〜を怖がる、恐怖を感じる

Women to protest the war. Alice made plans to travel to the Netherlands with her.

Alice Hamilton and Jane Addams arrived at The Hague, Netherlands, just as the first session was about to* open. Twelve warring and neutral nations were represented at the eleven-hundred-person congress. Most of the women, including the Americans, were not allowed to vote in their own countries. They may have had no part in declaring the war, but they would do anything they could to stop it.

When Jane Addams was asked to visit government leaders in France, Germany, Austria-Hungary, Italy, Holland, and Switzerland, Alice went along* as her unofficial companion. Disappointed but not really surprised when these personal appeals failed to end the war, Alice returned to the United States. There was nothing she could do to protect the soldiers, but there was another group of people she might be able to help. More determined than ever, she turned her attention to workers in the rapidly growing munitions, or weapons, industry.

---

*61　be about to　（まさに）〜しようとする
　　　例）I was just about to go out.
　　　　　私はちょうど出かけるところでした。
*62　go along　一緒に行く、同行する

⑤
Dangers Above and Below

Pursued by a cloud of foul-smelling, red smoke, Alice fled across the field. She felt choked by the fumes, and she gasped for breath.*⁶³ But she did manage to outrun the dangerous smoke from the picric acid factory. The hazardous chemical was used to make ammunition.

Alice found herself among the withered stalks of a cornfield. The men who had once farmed the land now worked in the factory making wartime chemicals. Although the United States had not yet entered World War I, Americans were helping to supply France with the explosives it needed. Factory accidents like this one had killed the remaining plants in the abandoned fields.

All around her, Alice saw workers who had hurried from the factory when the poisonous

---

＊63　gasp for breath　苦しそうに息をしている

45

fumes had begun to fill the building. Most of them had been stained yellow from daily exposure to the picric acid. Because of their coloring, the workers were called "canaries" by the townspeople.

Alice had seen her first canaries only a few hours earlier at a New Jersey railroad station. As she watched the terrible cloud dissolve in the sky, she remembered the man she had met at the station. This canary was a black man with bright orange nails, hair, and eyebrows. A yellow pallor covered his cheeks. The palms of his hands were dyed a vivid yellow. "Is the factory dangerous?" Alice had asked.

"Not the yellow stuff ain't," he replied, "but there's a red smoke comes off when the yellow stuff is making, and it like to knocks you out, and if you don't run, it gets you. You don't suspicion nothing much, you goes home and eats your supper and goes to bed, and then in the night you starts to choke up, and by morning you're dead."

Alice found the same bleak conditions in other factories. At a smokeless-powder factory in Virginia, she watched explosive particles being poured from a large pipe into a bin. They looked harmless, but her guide explained that sometimes sparks were produced when the particles rubbed together. If that happened, he warned, she should run for the nearest window. Alice stared. Jump out of a third-floor window? Then she saw the long safety chute leading to the ground. Fortunately she didn't have to use it.

Alice wanted to study army and navy arsenals as well as privately owned factories. The army welcomed her inspections of its manufacturing and storage sites, but the navy refused to grant her permission.

Finally Alice arranged an interview with the assistant secretary of the navy in Washington. The young man listened to Alice very carefully, then called a high-ranking admiral into the meeting. Soon Alice received the permission she needed. Thanking the assistant secretary for his speed and efficiency, Alice never dreamed that the man, Franklin Roosevelt, would one day be president of the United States.

After the United States entered the war in April 1917, Alice's work became even more demanding. Almost overnight, explosives manufacturers were required to increase production. But Alice soon noticed a more important change that could not be measured in numbers. The munitions workers' health was suddenly a matter of national concern.

Factories needed their employees to stay healthy[*64] in order to produce more weapons. As a result, doctors began to take a real interest in workers' welfare. Lawmakers and doctors began to talk about Alice's work and the solutions she was suggesting.

After the war, the interest in munitions workers' health spread to other industries. Industrial medicine was recognized as[*65] a respected branch of science, and Alice Hamilton was often credited as its pioneer. There were still hazardous jobs left to explore, and new ones were created as technology continued to develop. But Alice's work would never be quite so difficult again.

Reflecting the new interest in workers' health, the Harvard University Medical School established a department of industrial hygiene. Doctors had to be trained to[*66] meet the challenges of this new field. But who would teach them? The dean of the school hoped that Alice Hamilton would. He offered her a position as assistant professor. If she accepted the job, she would be the first female faculty member at the famous university.

But Alice liked working for the Labor Department and was not interested in studying department stores, as the dean had suggested.

---

*64　stay healthy　元気でいる、健やかでいる
*65　be recognized as　〜であると認められている
*66　be trained to　〜するように訓練する、教育する

Postponing her decision, she turned her thoughts to her upcoming investigation of Arizona copper mines.

On a chilly January morning in 1919, Alice set off from Hull House for one of the best adventures of her career. She was almost fifty years old. She looked and dressed like a young grandmother. But soon Alice found herself doing things few grandmothers would care to imitate.

In the Globe-Miami mining district of Arizona, she traded her long skirt for overalls and a helmet with a built-in lamp. Bravely she stepped into a "cage," which must have seemed a strange name for an elevator without walls. Alice had nothing to cling to as the cage lowered her shakily into the depths of the Old Dominion Mine. Eight hundred feet below the surface of the earth, the elevator came to rest.

Now Alice's adventure really began. Following her guide, she climbed up*67 a slope on her hands and knees to watch the miners operate their jackhammers. With these heavy machines, they drilled into*68 the tunnel walls in search of*69 copper. Some miners had reported that the powerful vibrations of the jackhammers were ruining their health. After a day in the mines, they felt sick*70 and weak.

---

*67　climb up　登る
*68　drill into　穴を開ける、掘り抜く
*69　in search of　〜を探す、探しに
*70　feel sick　吐き気がする、体調が悪い

49

Alice watched them carefully, noting that some of the jackhammers had water attachments to dampen the rocks. Miners could then drill without raising as much dust. But the men had not complained to* Alice about the dust. It was the vibrations of the jackhammers that they believed were making them sick.

Alice explored the entire mine. She climbed down an eighty-foot ladder into one pit. She crawled across another pit on a high railing. The rungs on the railing were so far apart that Alice had to stretch to reach them. One false move and she was sure she would fall into the blackness below. Forcing herself to remain calm,* she slowly and carefully followed her guide.

When Alice emerged into the daylight, she was certain that dust posed a greater threat to the miners' health than the jackhammers. At other mines and at meetings with workers and doctors, she urged more widespread use of the wet drill. She told them that she had tried the jackhammer and found it extremely uncomfortable, but she did not know if the vibrations alone could cause permanent injury.

A study of department-store workers could never compare with her experience in Arizona. And

---

*71　complain to　不平を言う、苦情を言う
*72　remain calm　冷静を保つ

yet as she headed home, Alice felt disappointed. She would have liked to teach at Harvard. It would have given her great satisfaction to train new doctors in industrial medicine.

To Alice's delight, she found a letter from Harvard awaiting her at Hull House. The university was offering her a half-time teaching appointment. This would leave her six months each year to work for the Labor Department. And she would not be required to*73 do the department-store study. Gratefully Alice sat down to write her acceptance.

---

*73　be required to　～するよう要請される

52

⑥
Lasting Contributions

Alice Hamilton and Jane Addams were crossing the ocean again. It was April 1919, the spring before Alice was to begin her duties at Harvard. The two women were on their way to the second International Congress for Women, in Zurich, Switzerland, to discuss the effects of the war.

When they arrived at the meeting, they heard shocking stories of children starving all over Germany. Until the defeated countries agreed to all the peace terms, the winning countries were preventing the delivery of food to Germany. Alice was saddened and angered by this food blockade. After the congress was over, she and Jane Addams toured the hungry nation for the American Friends Service Committee, a Quaker organization dedicated to providing food for the needy.

The children Alice met were pale and weak. At

a care center near Frankfurt, she saw schoolchildren eating lunch. They were so thin she could count their ribs, but all they had to eat was soup made mostly of water with a few grains and chopped leaves in it. Alice resolved to take the problem home to the people of the United States. If only*74 she could make her fellow citizens see the children through her eyes, she was certain they would be willing to help.

Back in Boston, Alice began teaching classes at Harvard. In her free time, she made speeches asking people to donate money to Quaker relief centers in Germany. But not everyone viewed the problem as she did. Many people still thought of the Germans as enemies. How could good Americans want to help their enemies? they asked.

Finally one university official asked Alice to stop her activities. People will not contribute to the school while there is a pro-German on the faculty, he explained. But who else would speak for the hungry German children? Alice kept right on asking for money.

She also kept right on visiting factories. When her official connection to the Labor Department ended in 1920, she continued her investigations with her Harvard colleagues. One important study

---

*74　if only…　〜でありさえすれば

54

involved the manufacture of felt hats, an industry in which large numbers of workers acted so strangely that they were called "mad hatters." Lewis Carroll had used the phrase humorously in his book *Alice in Wonderland*. But this real-life Alice knew there was nothing funny about the trembling limbs and irritable behavior of the sick men, exposed to deadly mercury nitrate every day. With her university associates, Alice worked to increase public awareness of this health menace. Gradually laws limited the use of mercury, and the felt-hat industry was pressured into[*75] replacing mercury nitrate with a nontoxic substance.

Alice's studies of mercury poisoning in the felt-hat industry and quicksilver mines, as well as her earlier government studies of industries in which carbon monoxide and aniline dye were used, helped pave the way for workers' compensation laws in several states. Under these regulations, men and women who were injured or became ill as a result of[*76] their jobs were entitled to[*77] financial support from their employers. Because manufacturers and insurance companies did not want to pay this extra money, they worked harder for safe, healthy factories.

Classes, field work, and other commitments

---

*75　pressure into　圧力をかけて〜（するように）させる
*76　as a result of　〜のために、の結果として
*77　be entitled to　〜する権利がある、権利を与えられる
　　例）They are entitled to join the meeting.
　　　　彼らはこの会議に参加する権利がある。

kept Alice almost constantly on the go.[*78] Between 1924 and 1930, she served as a member of the League of Nations Health Committee. After her first league meeting in Geneva, Switzerland, she toured the Soviet Union for a firsthand look at its industrial hygiene. And in 1925, she published a highly praised six-hundred-page textbook on industrial medicine.

After her retirement from Harvard in 1935, Alice went to live with her sister Margaret and a friend in Hadlyme, Connecticut. At sixty-six years old, Alice was energetic and keenly aware of what still needed to be done. She renewed her association with the Department of Labor and studied the viscose rayon, or artificial silk, industry. Based on her work, the Pennsylvania legislature passed its first workers' compensation law.

When she wasn't traveling, Alice enjoyed the community life at Hadlyme and took an active interest in the small town's affairs. She liked to garden and to chat with friends. She did not feel like an important or famous person at all.

One day Eleanor Roosevelt spoke at Connecticut College, near Hadlyme. Alice still treasured her memory of Franklin Roosevelt as the assistant secretary who had helped her during World War I.

---

*78　on the go　忙しく活動して、絶えず動き回り

56

She had a deep respect for Eleanor Roosevelt as well, because of Mrs. Roosevelt's commitment to helping others.

For the same reason, Mrs. Roosevelt admired Alice. Before her speech, she asked Alice to sit on the speaker's platform with her. Alice was flustered. "Nonsense," she replied. "I'm just a guest." Declining the spotlight, she chose to remain hidden in the audience with a friend.

Many years later, that friend described Alice as a person who "didn't want to be in the center of things." But when there was a cause she believed in, Alice was not shy. Then she did want to be at the center of things.

"I wouldn't change my life a bit," she once said, looking back on her long career. "Taking part in a new and expanding discipline brings out[*79] the best in one. For me the satisfaction is that things are better now, and I had some part in it."

Others were mindful, too, of the important part Alice played. She received many awards and honors through the years. In 1947 she was named New England Medical Woman of the Year and was given the prestigious Lasker Award by the U.S. Public Health Service. In honor of[*80] her ninetieth birthday, the Alice Hamilton Fund was

---

*79　bring out　（才能などを）引き出す
*80　in honor of　〜を祝して、〜に敬意を表して

set up[*81] at the Harvard School of Public Health. Two years later, a dormitory at Connecticut College was named after[*82] Alice and her sister Edith, who had become a famous writer.

But perhaps one of Alice's least expected and most moving compliments came just seven years after her retirement. As she and a guest entered the Department of Labor's private dining room in Washington, everyone in the room stood up in silent tribute. Afterward the government officials stopped by[*83] her table to greet her personally.

Even in retirement, Alice was guided by her mother's advice. Whenever there was something that needed to be done, Alice was ready to do it. One of her last public stands was to sign a protest against American involvement in Vietnam. Alice was ninety-four years old. As long as she lived, her determination to create a better world would never waver.

---

*81　set up　設立された
*82　name after　～の名をとって、名にちなんで
*83　stop by　立ち寄る、訪れる

59

Afterword

On February 27, 1969, Alice Hamilton, propped up[*84] in bed and wearing a pink nightgown, greeted a six-person delegation from the Women's International League for Peace and Freedom. It was her one-hundredth birthday, and people from all over the country were calling her and sending flowers and cards. Even President Nixon sent a telegram thanking Alice for her "lasting contributions to the well-being of our people and of men and women everywhere." Some friends baked a birthday cake for her. It had six roses and one bright candle.

Alice's mind wandered a good deal[*85] during her last years. Sometimes it was difficult to know what she was thinking. As she celebrated her birthday, she might have been remembering the

---

*84 prop up　もたれる、寄りかからせる、支える
*85 a good deal　たくさんの
　　例）I learned a good deal at highschool.
　　　私は高校でたくさんのことを学んだ。

children at Hull House, her peace missions to Europe, or any of her countless visits to dangerous factories.

The workers she had met in those factories were old now, too. Some would have grandchildren or even great-grandchildren old enough to have jobs. Wherever they worked, the new generations benefited from Alice's studies. She had helped create a new atmosphere in which industry and medical science cooperated to protect workers.

Alice Hamilton died in September 1970. That December a federal law was passed that gave the government the right to enforce health standards in privately owned businesses. Thanks to Alice's dedication and hard work, men and women in all sorts of jobs could look forward to the same kind of healthy, active old age that she herself had enjoyed.

Select Bibliography

Books

Grant, Madeleine P. *Alice Hamilton: Pioneer Doctor in Industrial Medicine*. New York: Abelard-Schuman, 1967.

Hamilton, Alice. *Exploring the Dangerous Trades: The Autobiography of Alice Hamilton*. Boston: Little, Brown, and Company, 1943.

Sicherman, Barbara. *Alice Hamilton: A Life in Letters*. Cambridge: Harvard University Press, 1984.

Articles

Felton, Jean Spencer, M.D. "Industrial Health as a Specialty: A Medical Field of Interest to Women's Physicians," *Journal of the American Medical Women's Association* (June 1947): 294-299.

Hamilton, Alice. "Pioneering in Industrial Medicine," *Journal of the American Medical Women's Association* (June 1947): 292-293.

Hamilton, Alice. "A Woman of Ninety Looks at Her World," *The Atlantic* (September 1961): 51-55.

———. "Edith and Alice Hamilton: Students in Germany," *The Atlantic* (March 1965): 129-132.

———. "Nineteen Years in the Poisonous Trades," *Harper's* (October 1929): 580-591.

Hardy, Harriet L., ed. *Journal of Occupational Medicine* (February 1972). Special issue dedicated to Alice Hamilton.

Sergeant, Elizabeth Shepley. "Alice Hamilton, M.D.: Crusader for Health in Industry," *Harper's* (May 1926): 763-770.

Urbano, Judy. "Doctor's Life Spanned Hull House, Labor Strife" and "Pioneering Doctor Made Hadlyme Her Last Home." Parts I, II. *The Gazette*, October 26 and November 2, 1978. (Courtesy of the Lyme Public Library, Lyme, Connecticut.)

———. "Dr. Alice Hamilton Celebrates 100th Birthday: Famed Industrial Toxicologist is Honored for her Work in Mines and Factories," Special to *The New York Times*, February 29, 1969.

Other sources include various newspaper and journal articles, biographical dictionaries, a biography of Edith Hamilton, and two doctoral dissertations.

訳者略歴

(監訳)

東　敏昭（ひがしとしあき）：産業医科大学学長。医学博士。昭和53年慶應義塾大学医学部卒業、昭和61年慶應義塾大学医学部講師（衛生学・公衆衛生学）、昭和63年産業医科大学産業生態科学研究所産業保健管理学准教授、平成元年カナダマクギル大学訪問准教授、平成4年産業医科大学産業生態科学研究所作業病態学教授（平成15～21年同研究所所長）、平成22年4月～平成26年3月　産業医科大学名誉教授・㈱デンソー北九州製作所経営管理部産業医・理事、平成26年4月より現職。中央じん肺審査医・日本産業衛生学会副理事長、他。

(訳)

吉村美穂（よしむらみほ）：梅光女学院大学短期大学部英米文学科卒業。産業医科大学産業生態科学研究所勤務。

働く人のための探偵
―― 米 産業医学の祖　女性医師アリス・ハミルトンを知っていますか？

平成12年4月1日	初版	定価（本体1,200円＋税）
平成14年9月10日	第2版	
平成19年3月10日	第2版第2刷	
平成27年3月1日	第3版	

著　　者　　ステファニー　サンマルチノ　マクファーソン
挿　　絵　　ジャネット　シュルツ
訳　　者　　東　敏昭、吉村美穂
編集発行人　岩﨑　伸夫
発　行　所　公益財団法人　産業医学振興財団
　　　　　　〒101-0048　東京都千代田区神田司町2-2-11　新倉ビル
　　　　　　TEL 03-3525-8291　FAX 03-5209-1020
　　　　　　URL http://www.zsisz.or.jp/
印　刷　所　株式会社　三和印刷社

ISBN978-4-915947-56-8 C2047 ¥1200E
©Toshiaki Higashi・Miho Yoshimura, 2016　落丁・乱丁はお取り替えいたします。
本書の全部または一部の複写・複製および磁気または光記録媒体への入力等を禁ず。